W9-DEX-874

The Gift of Morning Star

by

Thomas Aquinas Devlin

Catholic Evangelism Press, Inc.
P.O. Box 1282
Boca Raton, FL 33429-1282
Phone (305)360-9331   Fax (305)421-9921

ISBN 0-9633843-0-9

Library of Congress Catalog Card Number: 92-073148

Published by Catholic Evangelism Press, Inc.
P.O. Box 1282, Boca Raton, FL 33429-1282

Printed and bound in the
United States of America
July 1992

DECLARATION

Since the abolition of Canon 1399 and 2318 of the former Code of Canon Law by Pope Paul VI in AAS 58 (1966) P.1186, publications about new apparitions, revelations, prophecies, miracles, etc., have been allowed to be distributed and read by the faithful without the express permission of the Church, provided they contain nothing contrary to faith or morals. Therefore no imprimatur is necessary.

Chapter 2 No.12 of the Second Vatican Council's "Lumen Gentium" reads as follows:

"The Holy Spirit distributes special gifts among the faithful of every rank. Such gifts of grace, whether they are of special enlightenment or whether they are spread more simply and generally, must be accepted with gratefulness and consolation, as they are specially suited to and useful for the needs of the Church. Judgement of their genuineness and their correct use lies with those who lead the Church and those whose special task is not indeed to extinguish the spirit but to examine everything and keep that which is good."

"Extinguish not the spirit. Despise not prophecies. But prove all things, hold fast that which is good." 1Th 5:19-21

DEDICATION

This book is dedicated to Jesus, Mary and Joseph.

ACKNOWLEDGEMENTS

I wish to thank my children, Mari, Maureen, Moira, Patrick, Andrew, Brid, Sinead and Cormac for their love, support and understanding during my long absence while writing this book.

Thanks also is due to Hi and to Herbert who gave me so much insight into "Morning Star." While alive they devoted their entire life to the vision. They kept faith and never faltered. A special thanks to Cea, Hi's widow who shared so many moments of joy and sorrow during those days in the desert. God bless you.

Thanks also to Father J. who's help on the NEW GARMENT has been inspiring. I keep your request for anonymity and cherish your input.

There are many more who should be mentioned, but in respect to their personal wishes, thanks are privately expressed.

CONTENTS

CHAPTER 1

A PILGRIM'S PERSPECTIVE

The reason for this writing is to put into perspective some of today's events from the point of view of an ordinary, quiet and private Roman Catholic.

As a Roman Catholic, I am not really everything I am supposed to be according to the 'new age' Catholics. I am happy. I disagree with divorce and believe that re-marriage is adultery. I believe in Jesus Christ. I believe in the Bible. I believe in the rosary. I believe that the Pope is the Vicar of Christ on earth and is the heir of Saint Peter. I believe in the Sacraments. I believe in angels and saints, (I even talk to my angel whose name is 'Joseph')! I believe in forgiveness. I believe in confessing my sins to a priest. I believe that Jesus is truly present in the Eucharist. So why write?

I believe that being a true Christian is the highest order to which any human being can achieve here on earth, and that being a true Roman Catholic is the highest order of Christianity! I believe that other true Christians are walking in the light of Christ.

We are all pilgrims on this earth as we journey toward our true home in eternity. We traditional Catholics are labelled as uninformed, rosary rattling, fear filled, misguided people living in the dark ages, indoctrinated by an ignorant group of Irish priests and nuns who came to America from a backward thinking and culturally impoverished and primitive island. Well, I thank God that I was born and dragged up in that country and so have inherited all those "faults." So why write?

Let me tell you about my parents first, and then you might better understand. Daddy was born in the northern Irish mountains of County Tyrone in 1879 and was one of seven children, a small family by Irish standards! Educated to less than the equivalent of a first year grammar school level, his reading skills were sub-normal, but acceptable in his locale and era. He wrote me one letter in 1950 which took him all day to write the not more than 40 words! From about the age of six he herded cows every day on the mountains of Pomeroy for the princely sum of 2 pence a week. He improved later.

He was a typical primitive 'mountainy' farmer, who was born in a typical whitewashed cottage (kitchen, which doubled as the master bedroom, and two bedrooms), with a thatched roof, and a typical half door. The doors and sashes were painted green, standard Irish Catholic colors. The dogs, cats, chickens, geese, ganders, hens, roosters, musicians, adults and children would invade the kitchen with equal propriety until Granny would loose patience and let fly with the broom. Usually everyone escaped; sometimes, however, a hen or rooster didn't fare very well. On those occasions the family fared well!

He was a worker. He was a drunkard. He was human, and perhaps this characteristic is what I loved most about him. He was a gambler, loved the cards, horses and dogs and anything on which he could gamble. He loved to hunt but was a poor gunman. He was tried once for the murder of a Black and Tan, but got off when the judge saw Mammy and a squad of wee ones tugging at her skirt come into the courthouse in Dungannon. Daddy told me he did not do it, and I believed him. The evidence they had against him was "very incriminating;" they found the murder weapon, a single barrel shotgun in a drain on his property. Daddy owned a double barrel shotgun, and might have shot two! He detested violence, lies and cheating.

He had a deep and immovable faith and he loved the Mass and the Rosary. Once he brought me with him to Dublin. I remember that first night we stayed at Miss Cleary's 'Rooming House' at 64 Lower Baggot Street. When we got there all the boarders were 'at the Rosary,' led by the venerable Miss Cleary. She looked around at us intruders and in full verbal holy steam said, "...the Lord is with thee...Pat is it?... blessed art thou among women..." A great sense of humor Daddy loved poetry and music, but couldn't carry a note in a bucket if he tried, but he did try.

Daddy was generous to a fault. He gave and forgave and he never criticized anyone. He loved and was loved, but not by everybody. In spite of all his many faults he had many less faults than I do. Was he a good man? No, he was the best, and I love him still.

What about Mammy? I did not know her. I don't remember her, and all I can tell you is hearsay and not heresy. She was the toast of Ireland for beauty, wit and practical jokes. She could sing, dance, play the piano, peel potatoes and pray with the bishop with equal ease. Nothing was ever too much for her, and Daddy told me that he never heard her say a bad word about anyone, including himself! She was a model Catholic and loved everyone, prayed for everyone and was loved by everyone. "I give thanks to my God, always making remembrance of her in my prayers, as I hear of her charity and faith that she has in our Lord Jesus and towards all the saints."[1]

She was 21 years Daddy's junior, but age was never a barrier. She did not know Daddy until their wedding day as it was a fixed wedding. They made up for it with 15 children. She was told to have no more after the tenth child, but women will be women; they never give a poor man a rest!

Near the end of her fifteenth pregnancy her health was not the best. She was moved to a nursing home in Dublin City some 100 miles away, a full day's journey from Dungannon. One of the last letters she ever wrote was to her local doctor in Tyrone from St. Jarlath's Nursing Home on March the 2nd 1939 which reads: "Well, here I am and not much information I can give you yet. The doctor called yesterday, he is not going to do anything for me until 17th inst. until Pat comes home, as he still considers the case serious. He asked me if none of the doctors ever told me anything about my heart. I told him my heart never troubled me only during "pregnancy." Sincerely, Winnie Devlin."

Who did she think she was kidding, "only during pregnancy! She was nearly always pregnant! Married in 1916, she had babies in '18, '19, '21, '22, '24, '25, '27, '28, '29, '30, '32, '33, '34, '36 (that was me), and '39. Don't you love her simplicity? But then we Irish are a very simple people.

Again, I did not know her, but I love her anyway. You see, I have another fault, I believe what I am told by those whom I love, trust and respect, especially when it is uplifting and in my heart I know it to be truth. This is practical faith.

Why do I write? After Mammy died, Daddy and I used to talk a lot during the long lonely evenings. He would tell me about the old days and what he remembered from the "old people." Since he was born in 1879, his "old people" were the generation of the great famine of the 1830's and 40's. His "old people" had suffered the cruelties and evictions of the infamous Captain Boycott and his fellow English landlord tyrants. (The same Captain from whence the term 'Boycott' gets its name). Famines, evictions, beatings, murder, death, emigration, wars, politics, language barriers, misunderstandings, music, weddings, wakes, dances, parties, moon, stars, sun, skies, ocean, lakes, rivers, puddles, butter, cheese, barley, bread, money, poverty, cows, sheep, shepherds, wolves, foxes, bridges, new roads, tar and the wireless were all typical of his non-personal subjects.

From the viewpoint of this simple farmer, I try to put into perspective what he would say today and try to correlate this sophisticated world to his primitive world. Where is Boycott? Is his evil spirit still with us? Who is in charge? To whom do we turn? Whom can we trust? Who is the authority? Have we advanced since the famine? Ask the Ethiopians. Have we advanced since Boycott? Ask the homeless. Have we advanced since 'primitive loneliness'? Ask the drug addicts and drunkards. Are radio and television the answer? Ask the run-aways. Are we more informed? Ask the modern high school 'graduate' or the 'intellectuals.'

It is considered "intellectual" today to disagree with the God of Revelation. It is considered "intellectual" to disagree with traditional teachings, especially those inspired oral traditions, and to look with disdain upon the inspired traditional written word of the Bible.

The "intellectuals" seek to replace the authority of the Church and establish "democracy" ("demon-ocracy"). They want to replace "faith" with "reason." Was it not by "faith" that Peter walked on the water, or was it by "reason?" We all must get out of our comfortable boat and walk by faith, being aware that to walk to the exclusion of others and the exaltation of self is a "sinker." These so called "intellectuals," however, have also decided that the Bible is fictitious.

Why do I write? I am criticized by those posing as "faithful" and "evangelical" and "kindly" and "christian" (small "c" please), while in actual fact they are wolves in sheeps' clothing. Until he died in 1954, I listened to my Daddy talk of the happenings back in 1830 right up to that present day with the ease and simplicity equal to the most learned men of today. He was a man of faith, of tradition, of simplicity, of human feelings and failings, and he was honest. Did he quote reams of scripture? No, he lived them. Every time he said the full Rosary (2 Signs of the Cross, Creed, 1 Our Father, 3 Hail Marys, 1 Glory, 15 Our Fathers, 150 Hail Marys and 15 Glorys) he said 777 verses of scripture without the 'trimmings'! (See Appendix 1). Add 30 verses more each time he recited the Angelus! When I hear "new catholics" criticize the poor, ignorant people for rattling their rosaries I know who the ignorant are and I pray a Rosary for them. Those "poor, ignorant people" saying one Rosary recite more scripture in one day than most of their critics recite in a week. "The prayer of a just man is of great avail."[2]

When the good priests, friars and monks of the early Church started assembling all the writings into one book, the Bible, they did so lovingly, devotedly and painstakingly, because they were inspired by the Holy Spirit. Relying on the inspired and true written word of God contained in the Bible, and relying further on the inspired and true oral word of tradition as taught by the Catholic Church, and consulting the uninspired and sometimes untrue words of modern journalism, I have attempted in the following pages to as briefly as possible state how an Irish traditional Roman Catholic might see the world today.

You are invited to join me and together we will start at the beginning of the Christian era, take a look at some of the political and economic prophecies fulfilled in the First Revolt of 66-70 A.D., and see how they relate today to the preparations for the Second Coming of Jesus Christ.

We will take an overview of our modern money system and at the coins minted in Israel during the First Revolt and then at the USA Dollar. We will show their similarity. The Shekel, although unknowingly to the Jews, professed Jesus Christ, Who for them was 'a stumbling block.' The Dollar of our era, although unknowingly to the Freemasons, professes Jesus Christ, even though it was designed by Freemasons in an attempt to profess Satan.

We will show that the economic system is truly 'rupted,' corrupt and bankrupt, and how political pawns are nothing more than the tools and advocates for the Antichrist. We will show that the Antichrist and his antichrists will be defeated, and we will show that God's faithful remnant will be victorious.

We will show that all things work together for good, for those who love the Lord, and that His mercy, love and joy are still attainable for those who seek Him. Peace through prayer, prosperity through prudence, love through humility, and joy through patience, is my prayer for all.

Before we begin, let us consider four simple questions.

1. If you were living at the time of Noah would you have made it to the ark?

2. If you were living at the time of Sodom and Gomorrah would you have escaped?

3. Could you have predicted the Flood?

4. Could you have predicted the destruction of Sodom and Gomorrah?

Is this a "doomsday" message? If you are standing in error, yes. If you are standing with Jesus Christ it is VICTORY. Let us first look at what Jesus

5

promised.

Jesus promised to those who overcame to the end that He would give them authority over the nations which will be the Government of God on earth.

As we shall see later on, Jesus is the Bright Morning Star and Mary, His Blessed Mother and our Mother too, is the Morning Star. She is the "heavenly messenger" who has been appearing very frequently in this century with profound prophecies of hope, warning, preparation and expectation. She has told us to pray "during these years which still separate you from the great jubilee of the year two thousand."[3] We are told in scriptures that "You will declare this fiftieth year (jubilee year) to be sacred and proclaim the liberation of all the country's inhabitants."[4] Since our Blessed Mother said "...I am asking you to consecrate to me all the time that still separates you from the end of this century of yours...In this period...there will come to completion that fullness of time which was pointed out to you by me, beginning with La Salette all the way to my most recent and present apparitions,"[5] we should take heed and be prepared at all times.

Those who take refuge in her Immaculate Heart receive the gift of Morning Star. Through them, the Woman of Genesis will put her heel on the head of the snake. Through them, the Government of God will rule the earth. Through them, Jesus Christ the King of kings will reign Supreme.

CHAPTER 2

THE PROMISE

Before the Second Coming of the Messiah, Jesus Christ, the whole world will see and know that the word spoken by God through the prophets is fulfilled, and that the enemies of God are made His footstool. When that day comes, all aspects of living will be in the hands of God's chosen people. Every word of God will be fulfilled from Genesis through Revelation, both literally and symbolically, line upon line, and precept upon precept.

What a great time for all the Christian believers and practitioners of the word. They will control all things on earth; governments, law and justice, money and finances, outer space and the ocean depths, as ordained by God in Genesis chapter one. No aspect of living will be outside their control, because God will have given His authority to His people and will, through Jesus Christ, place the Government of God upon their shoulders.

During this present generation, fantastic advancements in technology have been achieved, and yet these are as naught in comparison to what is about to happen. Things which the eye has not yet seen, nor the ear yet heard, will hurtle the world into a new and exciting era. All those on the outside of this Kingdom of God-living will want to become part of the glory that has been foretold from the ancient days by The Ancient of Days.

There is to be a great revival in the churches. Church leaders will read with renewed vigor, insight and urgency, the messages of Revelation. This is the generation spoken of by the prophet Isaiah, the "Repairer of the breaches, and the restorer of paths to dwell in."[6] The spirit of repentance, forgiveness and love shall flourish. Parents will be reconciled to their children and the children to their parents. Nation will reconcile to nation and the evil spirit of lies and deceit will be overcome. Truth will prevail and all the people of the world will become one in the Lord. The promise of Genesis 3:15 will be fulfilled and the Woman Clothed with the Sun will have crushed the head of the serpent. This will be a glorious time of "kingdom living" and the prayer which the faithful have recited for over 1960 years, the prayer Jesus has taught us, will be answered; "Thy kingdom come."

In these present days there is a great loss of faith which is called "the great apostasy." Because of the astounding technology and ease of living, man once again thinks himself superior to God, and has turned away from God's blessings and graces. Ascending the technological 'tower of Babel,' man has denied God and put his trust in lifeless idols. Man wants money to buy things yet seeks not the greater things which money cannot buy.

A deceptive and cruel leader is about to come on the world scene who thinks he does not need God and will establish his own dominion. In his greed and lust for power he will try to dominate the world and set up his evil government, "The New World Order." This man is the pawn of Satan and totally possessed by Satan, and will lead even some of the elect astray. This man is the Antichrist, and will lead the world to the final battle of the ages, the battle of Armageddon.

A remnant of saints will remain true to Jesus Christ and will not be deceived by the initial false promises and easy compromises of 'the world.' This remnant of saints will suffer many hardships for the faith and will persevere to the end; they shall not be moved. They are resolute and courageous in their work, they are not afraid or disheartened, because the Lord our God is with them. He will not fail them nor forsake them before they have finished all the work to be done for the house of the Lord.[7] They are the victorious. As the Antichrist is being dispossessed, the world will look at the faithful remnant and say, "The Lord hath done great things for them."[8] The Antichrist and his followers will be defeated, not by arms, nor by might, but by the Spirit of the Living God. "The saints shall rejoice in glory...a two-edged sword in their hands, to execute vengeance upon the nations, chastisements among the people, to bind their kings with fetters, and their nobles with manacles of iron. To execute upon them the judgement that is written, this glory is to all His saints."[9]

After the defeat of the Antichrist the world will live in peace and tranquility. Then will begin the Glorious Reign of the victorious children of God here on earth who will live for ever and ever in the presence of the Creator of all things. There will be no tears, no sorrow, no hurt, no lies, no deceit, no sin and no decay. Only love will prevail, and God, who gave us His only begotten Son Jesus, will unfold the mystery and the vastness of the entire universe and heaven, in which the saints will live forever.

As God makes "known to us the mystery of His will according to His good pleasure,"[10] we come to understand some of the mystery and meaning of the Annunciation by the Angel Gabriel to Mary. For Catholics an understanding of our Blessed Mother is natural and necessary in gaining full knowledge of the story of salvation. It is difficult for us to accept the Protestant position of almost indifference, as we feel that they are missing a beautiful "advocate" in Mary. Some of my brothers in Christ are of the opinion that at the time of the Reformation, a lot of bitterness and hasty words planted seeds of hatred, distrust, distortion, doubt and false positions. Today, some of those ideas still remain and we pray that they will be overcome in the kindness, mercy and love of Jesus. On the other hand, most Protestants have come to believe that Mary is exclusively for Catholics, and that Catholics keep her as their own. Not so. We are all one body and have need of each other. Please understand this one point. With all the strength and sincerity of heart I love and reach out to all men, Protestant, Catholic and others to just once call Mary, "Blessed." Let us see how the story of Mary unfolds.

"In the beginning God created heaven..."[11] In this creation of Heaven, and it follows the heavenlies, that is the angels, God made known the creation of man. God revealed to the immortals (angels) that He was going to create mortals (man). He further told the immortals that they would serve the mortals who, at the end of the ages, would join them immortally for ever in Heaven. Some objected, some did not. "And there was war in Heaven. Michael and his angels battled with the dragon (Lucifer), and the dragon fought and his angels, and they did not prevail; neither was their place found any more in Heaven."[12] In short he was kicked out of heaven.

When Satan was cast out of Heaven, he lost further entry there. He could approach the outside of the gates of Heaven, but never again enter. "Now on a certain day when the sons of God came to stand before the Lord, Satan also was present among them."[13] In holding court OUTSIDE the gates, Satan was present to accuse the people on earth. It is important to emphasize that he did not go inside the gates; he therefore did not know what was going on INSIDE Heaven. He knew about earth, but not Heaven; "I have gone 'round about the earth, and walked through it."[14]

After God made man, Satan overcame man and God told him "I will put enmity between thee and the woman, and thy seed and her seed; she shall crush thy head, and thou shalt lie in wait for her heel."[15] Satan thought that by contaminating woman the entire human reproduction would be contaminated with sin. God knew differently. In Heaven He divulged His plan to His angels, for the salvation of mankind. Since Satan was already expelled, he had no access and therefore he did not know God's plan.

The angels were awestruck at His plan, His wonder and His mercy. The idea that He should espouse an IMMACULATE woman, a mortal, conceive the Son in her through the Holy Spirit, and carry out the perfect sacrifice through her and WITH her is one of the greatest of Biblical wonders. "And

9

thy own soul a sword shall pierce, that the thoughts of many hearts may be revealed."[16]

The generations failed to keep God's law from Adam down to Lamech, the father of Noah. "Noah was a just and perfect man...he walked with God."[17] The twelfth generation from Noah is Abraham, and the third after that is Jacob.[18] The prophecy in Genesis begins to be more fully revealed in Jacob's time. "And he saw in his sleep a ladder standing upon the earth, and the top thereof touching Heaven, the angels of God ascending and descending by it, and the Lord leaning upon the ladder, saying to him: 'I am the Lord God of Abraham thy father, and the God of Isaac; the land wherein thou sleepest, I will give to thee and to thy seed...and IN THEE and thy seed all the tribes of the earth SHALL BE BLESSED.'"[19] These angels were to be seen again ascending and descending at the birth of Jesus.

When Jacob obtained his father's blessing, Isaac said: "Be thou lord of the brethren (brothers) and let thy mother's ('other' as in the New Jerusalem bible) brothers bow down before thee."[20] This is the same of whom the prophet Balak spoke; "I see Him - but not in the present. I perceive Him - but not close at hand. A STAR is emerging from Jacob, a septre is rising from Israel."[21]

Isaiah says "Behold a virgin shall conceive and bear a Son, and His name shall be called Emmanuel."[22] He reveals in prophetic timing "a CHILD IS BORN to us, and a Son IS given to us, and the Government IS upon His shoulder,"[23] and "The Lord sent a WORD into Jacob, and it hath lighted upon Israel."[24]

Now let us put all this in Marian context but with the emphasis on the theology of history, and understand a little more clearly "The Holy Spirit" and the words of Gabriel. "Who is the Holy Spirit?: The flowering of the love of the Father and the Son. If the fruit of created love is a created conception, then the fruit of Divine Love, that prototype of all created love, is necessarily a divine 'CONCEPTION.' The Holy Spirit is, therefore, the 'uncreated eternal CONCEPTION,' the prototype of all conceptions that multiply life throughout the whole universe."[25]

To make way for God's plan, it was necessary to prepare an IMMACULATE ark which was without spot or blemish to carry the infant Jesus. When Joachim and Ann conceived Mary in the natural way of man and wife, the union formed Mary. This was the moment of the IMMACULATE conception. This was different from all other conceptions.

10

Through the power of the Holy Spirit, Satan was not allowed to enter the gates of God's temple! Mary was the creation and the spouse of the Holy Spirit. Satan therefore, was not allowed to enter this temple with original sin. This was not an ordinary woman, one who would not have an ordinary son, and would, therefore, be a light, a star, for all generations.

The Archangel Gabriel was sent to visit the IMMACULATE virgin Mary and was told exactly what to say by the Father: "Hail, full of grace, the Lord is with thee. Blessed art thou among women...The Holy Spirit shall come upon thee and the power of the Most High shall overshadow thee; and therefore the Holy One to be born shall be called the Son of God."[26] The "Hail Mary" is an exact prayer from God the Father, offering and asking her to be the mother of His only Begotten Son.

"There was silence in Heaven for about half an hour"[27] as the Divine Trinity and all the angels waited for Mary's answer. She questioned, pondered in her heart and then said "Behold the handmaid of the Lord, be it done unto me according to Thy word."[28] Imagine how the cheers and alleluias chorused in Heaven!

At that time the most awesome event took place. Jesus, the Second Person of the Blessed Trinity departed Heaven, yet never leaving the Father's side. As the stunned angels looked on, their God became an infinitely small spiritual seed which was transmitted by the Holy Spirit and planted in the womb of Mary. At that moment "The Word became flesh." She thus became the espoused of the Holy Spirit, and took the powerful name of her own conception as a dutiful bride should do, "The IMMACULATE CONCEPTION."

Because Satan was not allowed to possess Heaven any more, so too he could not possess the espoused of Heaven who had to be, by definition, 'IMMACULATE,' both in conception and in conceiving. Furthermore, he did not know Who was in Mary's womb, for if he did he would not have said to Jesus: "IF You are the Son of God..."[29] Satan's followers would not have had Him crucified had they known Who He was. "We speak the wisdom of God, mysterious, hidden, which God foreordained before the world...a wisdom which none of the rulers of this world has known; for had they known it, they would never have crucified the Lord of Glory."[30]

Mary is at the same time the daughter of the Father, the mother of the Son and the spouse of the Holy Spirit. She was chosen by the Father, she was chosen for the Son.

11

She is the WOMAN foretold in Genesis 3:15. On the cross Jesus said to His mother, "WOMAN behold, thy son." At the foot of the cross, Saint John represented all of us. The other disciples had either fled, denied or betrayed Jesus. The only one remaining to receive the message from Jesus was John, "Behold thy mother."[31] In describing the scene beneath the cross it is interesting to note that John uses the word "MOTHER" five times in three verses while talking about Mary, and when Jesus addresses His mother from the cross for the last time He calls her "WOMAN." He was fulfilling yet another prophecy. Mary is the WOMAN foretold in Genesis, she is the WOMAN foretold in Canticles, she is the WOMAN at the foot of the cross, she is the WOMAN of the Apocalypse! Our Blessed Mother will crush the head of the serpent to which the first mother, Eve, succumbed. Jesus had already crushed Satan on the Cross, Adam fell into the temptation which Jesus overcame for us. Jesus saved man all the way back to Adam.[32]

Mary is the **ARK OF THE NEW COVENANT** for in her womb she carried the Word, the Bread of Life and the Branch.[33]

Mary is **THE GATE OF HEAVEN**. Mary is the gate through which the Father reached us. Mary, the ladder in Jacob's dream[19], is the Gate of Heaven.

Mary is **THE EAST GATE**. "And behold the glory of the God of Israel came in by way of the east...and the majesty of the Lord went into the temple by the way of the gate that looked to the east... And the Lord said to me: This gate shall be shut, it shall not be opened, and no man shall pass through it because the Lord, the God of Israel, hath entered in by it, and it shall be shut for the Prince."[34] Mary, the gate through which the Prince entered, is the EAST gate, which God opened. Further if we study the geography and plan of the Temple we will see that the Women's court was to the EAST, and entry to it was through the "Beautiful Gate."

Mary is **THE MORNING STAR**. Jesus is **"THE BRIGHT MORNING STAR."**[35] Mary is the star spoken of in Numbers,[21] she is the Morning Star in Re 2:28. Saint Paul tells us that "star differs from star in glory."[36] Astronomy teaches that the morning star is a cluster of stars making up the one unit which we call the "morning star." In understanding the scriptural "morning star," it is necessary to understand all that is contained in the promise by Jesus. Let us follow Mary to Jesus.

When the three wise men followed the star from the EAST, it came to rest over the stable in Bethlehem, "And entering the house they found the Child

12

with Mary His mother, and falling down they worshipped Him."[37] So also do wise men today find Jesus with Mary!

Mary is the perfect temple created by the Holy Spirit, and we are the temple of the Holy Spirit.[38] We are the body of Christ.[39] Christ is the Head of the Body.[40] The body, therefore, has to be formed in the same womb as the head. Because Jesus said to Mary: "Woman, behold thy son." and to John: "Behold, thy mother," it is then in her spiritual womb that the Body of Christ (that is, us) must be formed.

Mary is the WOMAN foretold in Canticles; "Who is she that cometh forth as the morning rising, fair as the moon, bright as the sun, terrible as an army set in array?"[41] It is Mary, the mother of the body of Christ! She will crush the head of the enemy and just as Joseph in Genesis was a foreshadow of Jesus, so too Judith was a foreshadow of Mary. "The Lord hath blessed thee by His power, because by thee He hath brought our enemies to nought...Blessed art thou, O daughter, by the Lord the most high God, above all women upon earth. Blessed be the Lord Who made heaven and earth, Who directed thee to the cutting off the head of the prince of our enemies...Blessed art thou in every tabernacle of Jacob, for in every nation which shall hear thy name, the God of Israel shall be magnified on occasion of thee."[42] And Mary replied, "My soul magnifies the Lord and my spirit rejoices in God my Savior, because He has regarded the lowliness of His handmaid, for behold, henceforth all generations shall call me blessed."[43]

Pope St. Sixtus (423-440) proclaimed that Mary is the Mother of God, following the decision reached by the Council of Ephesus (431). Pope Pius XII (1936-'58) proclaimed as Church Doctrine (dogma) in 1950, that Mary was assumed body and soul into heaven, and that she is Queen of Heaven and earth, angels and men. This inspired oral tradition is scriptural; "So then brethren, stand firm, and hold the teachings that you have learned whether by word or letter of ours."[44] In these proclamations Satan is truly defeated by the WOMAN. Thanks to the Son and guided by the Holy Spirit, Holy Mother Church flourishes.

"The dead men shall live, My slain shall rise again: awake and give praise, ye that dwell in the dust, for thy dew is the dew of light, and the land of the giants thou shalt pull down into ruin."[45] In Daniel it is prophesied "many of those that sleep in the dust of the earth shall awake...they that are learned shall shine as the brightness of the firmament and they that instruct many to justice, as stars for all eternity."[46] We are told in Matthew that "the tombs were opened, and many bodies of the saints who had fallen

13

asleep arose, and coming forth from the tombs after His resurrection...came into the city and appeared to many."[47] One of those now appearing to the world is Mary, the Mother of Jesus, who died and was assumed body and soul into Heaven. (This could not be otherwise since she was IMMACULATE and knew no sin as we shall see in Chapter 12). She is presently appearing and is instructing "many to justice." Her messages today to all the world are the same as when she said to the servants "Do all that He tells you."[48] They are; TURN TO JESUS, DO ALL THAT HE TELLS YOU, READ THE HOLY SCRIPTURES, pray the Rosary, attend Holy Mass, fast and go to Confessions monthly.

These prayers and works are necessary. By reading and understanding the scriptures, by hearing and knowing the word of God, we know that Satan is a liar and a thief, and even though he is persuasive and deceptive in implanting his evil spirit of pride, arrogance, corruption, confusion, voodoo, bribery, hatred, murder, lust, greed, envy etc., he is uncovered. He is a cunning, persistent, evil and relentless serpent, who is succeeding in turning many people from God, to revolt against Him, to apostatize.

We have entered the era of the Great Apostasy. There are a number of startling and urgent events happening today which have ushered in the "end times." Most people are unaware of their role in sacred history and the significance today of certain economic and political events which are a fulfillment of those things prophesied from the beginning of the world. For the sake of brevity, we shall start in the early years of the Christian era. There was so much prophecy contained in that 'First Revolt' of 66 A.D., so much suffering by the Jews and so much faith. In spite of betrayal and seeming defeat, they persisted. That revolt in 66 by the forces of good will have many similarities with the current forces of good against the revolt by the 666 forces of evil.

In Chapter 3 let us begin at 66 A.D.

CHAPTER 3

THE SHEKEL OF ISRAEL

Under severe oppression, the Jews revolted in 66 A.D. with such ferocity and determination that they almost toppled the mighty Roman Empire. While striking their blow for freedom, and in order to assert their total independence from pagan Rome, they set up their own government which included establishing their own currency and minting their own coin, the silver Shekel of Israel.

If we examine these coins for their prophetic, symbolic and historical values, we will see why they are a reminder to all the truthful and faithful that the world will once again return to God's way, to His system of government and to His golden standard.

The obverse, or front of the coin has a chalice with the Hebrew inscription SHEKEL OF ISRAEL. The chalice symbolizes the blood of the covenant between God and Abraham, and to all disciples of Christ it symbolizes the new covenant of the blood of Jesus, Son of God, for the salvation of all. Because sacrificial blood of animals sealed the old covenant,[49] the sacrificial blood of our Spotless and Innocent Redeemer sealed the new covenant.[50]

Year 1   Year 2   Year 3   Year 4   Year 5

The reverse side of the coin has three distinct parts which are joined together in unity. Three pomegranates are each joined by the stem to the branch. The Hebrew inscription reads JERUSALEM THE HOLY.

15

"Jerusalem The Holy" is taken from Scriptures. "I am appointed king by Him over Zion His holy mountain."[51] Zion is the name that has always been applied to Jerusalem. "Solomon then summoned the elders of Israel to Jerusalem to bring the ark of the covenant of the Lord up from the City of David, that is Zion"[52] and again, "Take pity on Your Holy City, Jerusalem, Your dwelling place,"[53] and finally, "Your oppressors' children will humbly approach you, at your feet all who despise you will fall addressing you as 'City of the Lord', 'Zion of the Holy One of Israel.'"[54]

For Christians, the names Israel, Jerusalem and Zion have particular symbolic meanings. They are:

ISRAEL is all God's people who have called on the name of the Lord.

JERUSALEM is all of those who live in an orderly and lawful arrangement called the Church.

ZION is the place of the law, the Roman Catholic Church. Peter built the administration according to the instructions (keys) given him by Jesus. "I will give thee the keys of the Kingdom of Heaven, and whatever thou shalt bind on earth shall be bound in Heaven, and whatever thou shalt loose on earth shall be loosed in Heaven."[55] Paul helped build the Church by the fire of the Holy Spirit. To the Romans he wrote, "I give thanks to my God through Jesus Christ for all of you, because your faith is proclaimed all over the world...For I long to see you that I may impart some spiritual grace unto you to strengthen you, that is, that among you I may be comforted together with you by that faith which is common to us both, yours and mine...For I am not ashamed of the gospel, for it is the power of God unto salvation to everyone who believes, to Jew first and then to Greek. For in it the justice of God is revealed, from faith unto faith, as it is written 'He who is just lives by faith.'"[56] The Holy Spirit through Peter and Paul moved the administration of the Church from Jerusalem to Rome. There has not been any inspired approval to remove it from Rome. It is still the seat of the true Church. The destruction of the Temple has a more significant meaning to Catholics than do the bricks and mortar to the Jews. The Holy Spirit moved the Church right into the heart of the then pagan Romans. There it has remained ever since, through persecutions, tribulations and expansion. The Church preaches in every language, in every tongue, and has been blessed with successors to Saint Peter. Pope John Paul II is the 265th pope, Saint Peter being the first. There have been 37 antipopes (all between the years 217 and 1449) who tried to take the Church for their own self aggrandizement. The first 14 of these anti-popes were between 217 - 903; 16 in the period 974 -1180 and 7 between 1338 and 1449.

The three pomegranates on the shekel, joined by the STEM to the BRANCH represent the TRINITY. We first see the Trinity when Abraham "...was sitting at the door of his tent, in the very heat of the day. And when he lifted up his eyes, there appeared to him three men standing near him. And as soon as he saw THEM he ran to meet THEM from the door of his tent, and adored down to the ground and said, 'Lord, if I have found favor in THY sight, pass not away from Thy servant.'"[57] He sees three men and addresses them in the singular "LORD"...the Trinity.

Two New Testament quotes on the Trinity will further help clarify the point. "Go, therefore, make disciples of all nations; baptize them in the name of the Father and of the Son and of the Holy Spirit,"[58] and "...who have been chosen in the foresight of God the Father, to be made holy by the Spirit, obedient to Jesus Christ and sprinkled with His blood."[59]

The three pomegranates, joined by the STEM to the BRANCH, are seen in "A shoot will spring from the STEM of Jesse, and a BRANCH from his roots will bear fruit,"[60]thus the direct introduction of Jesus, who was born of the tribe of Judah, from the stem of Jesse and the branch of David[61]...the stem and the branch of the three fruits. "The Lord of hosts says this: Here is a Man whose name is Branch; where He is there will be a branching out and He will rebuild The Lord's sanctuary."[62] This is fulfilled and confirmed by Jesus, "I am the root and the offspring of David, the Bright Morning Star."[35] We shall see this prophecy further expanded in Chapter 10 when examining the Government of God and places of refuge.

The branch of three pomegranates is in transition from flower to fruit, from the Law to fulfillment, from the vineyard to the harvest, from the promise to the first fruits, from earth to Heaven. He came and bore witness among us and He is the First Fruit by His resurrection from the dead. "He is the Head of His body, the Church, He Who is the beginning, the First Born from the dead, that in all things He may have first place."[63]

Throughout scripture we have many references to the harvest, and it is the most common term for bringing souls into the kingdom of God, "Then He said to His disciples, 'The harvest is rich but the laborers are few, so ask the Lord of the harvest to send out laborers to His harvest."[64] The harvest referred to in the coins is the harvest for which The Messiah wants us all to work...souls. This harvest of souls represented by the trinity of pomegranates will be seen again in the war against Iraq, when the Israel was included by political means.

The year of 'independence' (or the year of the revolt as it turned out to be) was identified on the obverse of the coins as 'Year 1,' 'Year 2' and so on for the five years of the revolt which was quashed in 70 A.D. A new coin was minted each year.

Compare the parallel events of the passion of Jesus to the First Revolt:

FIVE PARTS OF THE PASSION THE FIVE YEARS OF THE REVOLT

1. The Agony in the garden.   1. 66 A.D. Revolt begins.
2. The scourging at the pillar.   2. 67 A.D. Betrayal by a few.
3. The crowning with thorns.   3. 68 A.D. Self determination.
4. The carrying of the cross.   4. 69 A.D. Revolt continues.
5. Crucifixion and death of Jesus. 5. 70 A.D. Revolt crushed and
                                     the Temple destroyed.

The Agony ended in death...then came the Resurrection for the believers!

The revolt ended in destruction...then came 'a big parenthesis' for the unbelievers!

Jesus said "Destroy this Temple and in three days I will raise it up...But He was speaking of the Temple of His body."[65]

Recall the destruction of the Temple in three days, just 40 years after the death of Jesus. (The Romans entered the temple on 8 August 70 and completely destroyed it on 10 August 70). When Jesus died the veil of the Temple was torn and all mankind had direct access to the Holy of Holies. Some Jews did not believe this. "...their minds were closed; indeed, until this very day, the same veil remains over the reading of the Old Testament: it is not lifted, for only in Christ is it done away with."[66] Jesus said that He came not to abolish the Law but to fulfill the Law.[67] When the Romans destroyed the Temple in 70 A.D., the Jews could no longer fulfill the Law for the expiation of sins under Leviticus.[68] Jesus had already fulfilled the Law. The Associated Press reported from Jerusalem on 9 May 1989 Rabbi Nahman Kahane of the Temple Institute as saying that "All Jewish history as far as we are concerned is one big parenthesis until the temple is returned." The unbelievers missed the message that the believers are the Temple. The rabbi was looking for the material things, the perishable building; God is looking for the imperishable, our souls, the real harvest, the real Temple. The Temple building which was destroyed in 70 A.D. was only a deed that the unbelieving could see, causing for them a 'big parenthesis.' The believing already knew The Way.

18

Jesus became The High Priest for all mankind and for ever and ever. In the 22nd Psalm which Jesus recited during His passion He said "...Dogs have surrounded Me; a band of evil men have encircled Me, they have pierced My hands and My feet. I can count all My bones; people stare and gloat over Me...The whole wide world will remember and return to The Lord, all the families of nations bow down before Him. For to The Lord, ruler of the nations, belongs kingly power! All who prosper on earth will bow before Him, all who go down to the dust will do reverence before Him. And all those who are dead, their descendants will serve Him, will proclaim His name to generations still to come; and these will tell of His saving justice to a people yet unborn, He has fulfilled it."[69] Jesus is the Temple that was raised up again on the third day, He has fulfilled it.

All mankind must remember that the Word of God is certain and true, that all His words will be fulfilled, line upon line and precept upon precept. When we look at the coins, remember:

1) The Romans were so incensed with the small nation which almost toppled their empire that the Jews were exiled after the revolt was suppressed a second time.

2) The name of the country was then changed by the Romans to the Latin name for Philistine, that is "Palestine" as a revenge for the revolt.

3) The Jews were in exile until 2 November 1917 when the Balfour Declaration was made in London, allowing the Jews to return.

4) On 9 December of that year the words of the prophet Isaiah were fulfilled, "As birds flying, so will the Lord of hosts protect Jerusalem, protecting and delivering, passing over and saving. Return as you had deeply revolted, O children of Israel."[70] The British RAF planes dropped leaflets from the sky over the city of Jerusalem, asking the then conquerors, the Turks and Germans, to withdraw peacefully without causing damage to the Holy City. They obeyed. The motto of General Allenby's 14th Bomber Squadron "as birds flying" over the city was "I spread my wings and keep my promise." The Jews have and are still returning to Jerusalem.

5) It was finally on 14 May 1948 that the name of "Israel" was restored to the Promised Land, thus finally bringing victory to the revolt of 66 A.D.

6) Until the Israelites finally won back the entire area of Israel in

19

1967, that is all of Jerusalem, the West Bank and the Gaza Strip, it was impossible for the" man of sin...the son of perdition" to be revealed. "And now you know what restrains him, that he may be revealed in his proper time."[71] Prophecy could not be fulfilled until all of Israel was a nation once again. Now that particular restraint is lifted.

We can see that the coins have prophetic, symbolic and historic values and we will now show that they are a reminder to all the truthful and faithful that the world will once again return to God's Way, to His SYSTEM OF GOVERNMENT and to His economic standard. "All estimation shall be made according to the shekel of the sanctuary."[72]

How does the First Revolt relate to today? Does it lead to any new events and developments? The answer is a definite YES. The center of the universe is Israel.[73] Not only does God say it, which of course makes it true, but also the Antichrist wants to set up his headquarters in Jerusalem prior to Armageddon.[74] Why would he do such a dumb thing when he is forewarned of the events? First he is arrogant and thinks he will win, and second, "none of the wicked shall understand, but the learned shall understand."[75]

Why are Israel, Jerusalem and the Israelites so important in history? The answer is simple. The Israelites are God's chosen people, Israel is the land He promised to them and Jerusalem is His Holy City. All Christians are spiritual Israelites.

The devil wants to control all these elements and so he wages war against all physical and spiritual Israelites. Because he would serve neither God nor man, he continues to set up his Babylon in defiance of God. Well, he cannot win because God has already won by the triumph over death and the glorious resurrection of Jesus Christ. However, that 1948 victory by Almighty God was countered when in another part of the world the U. S. Supreme Court started to hand over the children of the USA to Satan.

The only consolation for the devil will be the number of souls he can lead to perdition. He does this by pride, arrogance, corruption, confusion, voodoo, bribery, hatred, murder, lust, greed, anger, sloth, envy, gluttony and all other forms of sin...Babylon![76] But Babylon must fall and the government of God must reign supreme over the fullness of the earth.

The Shekel prophesied some of events which have happened in the political and economic areas, let us now examine the USA dollar and it's connection to the economic and political Babylon.

20

CHAPTER 4

THE USA DOLLAR BILL

America is a great country. She is the home of the brave, the land of the "free." America is beautiful for spacious skies, and amber fields of grain. She opened her doors and accepted the poor, the weary and the despised of the world. They came and they loved her. They built her and suffered with her. She became for them 'the land of milk and honey.' I am an Irishman and I say "America, I love you from sea to shining sea. I love your people. I love your Spirit. I love you!"

America, however, is the most maligned of nations. Why? The "New World" has suffered and is in agony. It is the center of a battle between Good and Evil. Good will win, but in the meantime let us look at some parts of the struggle and realize what we must do to win. We know that in Jesus victory is assured from the cross, so let us not perish for a lack of knowledge.

"Love of money is the root of all evil,"[77] so then let us look at the one dollar bill with it's "Great Seal of the United States of America" inscription. Let us look at it from the perspective that it has been contaminated with the influence of Freemasonry. Although we shall deal with the Masons in greater detail later on, let us look at a few definitions which will help in understanding their voodoo.

According to Father Bradley S.J., "Masonry is a peculiar system of morality, veiled in allegory and illustrated by symbols." This quasi-definition will help us to see Satanism in operation. It is veiled in that it acts in the shadows behind 'front-men,' and through them makes itself heard. Front men by and large are politicians and political clergymen.

To most Masons their god is a god of geometry, as is evidenced by their symbols, compass, set square, and pyramid overseen by the satanic "Eye of Providence." They call this god "The great architect of the universe." This is not the One True God of Revelation.

Mason's 'god' is 'humanism,' that is, the natural knowledge of the human mind. This becomes self-appreciation and leads to the self-worship and idol-worship of man, contrary to the second commandment. There is no dependence on God since secular thought is their 'god.' This humanism becomes "Secular Humanism" and revolts against God.

If we examine the dollar bill with the above brief introduction to Freemasonry, we will have a new insight. Ben Franklin (1706-90) is unquestionably one of the earlier masters of the US currency. This revered man in American history was elected Grand Master of the Freemasons in Philadelphia in 1736. In 1782, eight years before his death, The Great Seal of the United States, which is on the dollar bill was designed.

When the dollar bill was redesigned in 1935, the Masonic symbol was put on its reverse. The Great Seal of the United States makes no direct overt reference to any Masonic symbolism as evidenced by former Vice President Henry A. Wallace, a Mason. When the new design for the US dollar bill was shown to President Franklin D. Roosevelt in 1935, FDR 'at first worried that using the Eye of Providence (the Masonic emblem atop the 13-step pyramid on the reverse of the Seal) would offend Catholics. After being assured by Post Master General James A. Farley, a Catholic, that it would not, Roosevelt gave the go-ahead.'[78] Roosevelt, like Wallace, was a 32nd degree Mason.[79]

When we examine The Great Seal we note on the obverse (front) the eagle, with 32 feathers on one wing and 33 feathers on the other. There are 32 degrees in Freemasonry, and 33 degrees in the Scottish Rite, the 33rd degree being the Supreme Command, the circle of "the illuminati, the enlightened!" Both inequalities are symbolized in the Great Seal.

There are nine tail feathers, and these represent the York (of England) rite of Freemasonry which has nine degrees...thus giving it the international and founding "status."

There are 13 stars in the crest.

There are 13 letters in the ribbon below entitled "E Pluribus Unum," From many, one. (All for Satan as they thought).
There are 13 bars in the shield.
There are 13 arrows.
There are 13 leaves on the olive branch.

The fact that there were 13 original states is secondary because they only allowed 13 states into the union to start with! Satan's number was the most important fact. 13 is the number assigned to Satan!! 13 in Sacred Numbers signifies treachery. In Genesis 14:5, the five kings revolted against the four in the thirteenth year. Just as Lucifer, (later to be called Satan by God), revolted against the universal (4 being the number for universal) authority of God, so too, Satan inspired the five, number for grace, to fall from grace and revolt in year 13.

On the reverse of the seal there is the pyramid with the Satanic Eye of Providence.

The pyramid has 13 granite stones! Here the author of confusion, Satan, confused even himself and his satanic worshippers. They say that these 13 steps represent the steps to Solomon's Temple. Not so. There were 15 steps to the Temple and these are well recorded in Jewish tradition when they said the 15 "gradual" Psalms by which they ascended to the Temple, that is Psalms 120 to 134.

There are three written captions, namely:
"MDCCLXXVI" (9 letters),
"Annuit Coeptis" (13 letters), and
"Novus Ordo Seclorum."
These are, of course, in Latin and are translated "1776," "New Beginnings" and "New World Order." This motto of secular humanism is the motto for the New World Order which by another definition is the "New Order of the Ages."

People may ask "Why bother with numbers?" This is a good question. NUMBERS are part of the Catholic Church's tradition, both oral and written, and are in accordance with the verse "Thou hast ordered all things in measure, and NUMBER and weight."[80] Father John Hardon, S.J. gives a brief outline of the meaning and source of religious numbers.[81] I have incorporated some of his work here.

1.	God, Father.
2.	There is Another. Two distinct natures in Christ, divine and human.
3.	Trinity. Divine.
4.	Universal. Four sides to man, Ark of the Covenant, Temple.
5.	Grace. Five wounds of Christ.
6.	Man, created on day 6, imperfection.
7.	Spirit, perfection.
8.	New Beginning
9.	Judgment. Nine choirs of angels.
10.	Order. Fullness.
11.	Disorder. Incomplete as evidenced by Judas' defection.
12.	Divine order (Government). Maturity.
13.	Treachery. "Recalling the presence of the traitor at the Last Supper, beyond Christ and the faithful eleven apostles."[81]
40.	Trials, testing or waiting.
50.	Divine fulfillment of a promise.
100.	Plenitude.
1,000.	An immense number. Eternity, "because all higher numbers are either an addition to a thousand or multiplications of the same."[81]

As Roman Catholics we and all other Christians claim the authority which Jesus Christ has given to us and by His power make all things subject to Him. With this God given authority, we claim the US Dollar for Jesus and invoke His measure and number according to His instructions. We recall, therefore, the words of the Psalmist "Their madness is according to the likeness of a serpent ...but Thou O Lord, shalt laugh at them, Thou shalt bring all the nations to nothing."[82]

How do we laugh at them? How do we 'claim' for Jesus Christ that which a nation has accepted? "Make friends for yourselves with the mammon of wickedness."[83] We will see later that the monetary system inaugurated by man must fail. In the meantime, we must use what is in place for the furtherance of the Kingdom of God. We do not become slaves to that mammon, but we use it for the Kingdom, remembering that "from the days of John the Baptist until now the Kingdom of Heaven has been enduring violent assault, and the violent have been seizing it by force."[84]

Because we are speaking of Freemasonry, whose god of wisdom is the serpent, we Catholics are reminded of the scriptural story of the fiery serpents. The Israelites spoke against God and Moses, whereupon "the Lord sent among the people fiery serpents, which bit them and killed many of

24

them. Upon which they came to Moses and said, 'We have sinned because we have spoken against the Lord and thee, pray that He may take away these serpents from us.' And Moses prayed for the people. And the Lord said to him, 'Make a brazen serpent, and set it up for a sign, whosoever being struck shall look on it, shall live.' Moses therefore made a brazen serpent, and set it up for a sign, which when they that were bitten looked upon, they were healed."[85] (Did you ever wonder why Catholics have images, or where the medical profession got it's emblem?)

Let us re-examine the US one dollar bill in the light of Jesus Christ! Neither the dollar nor The Great Seal of the United States belong to the Satanic Freemasons, they belong to Jesus Christ the Messiah, as does the United States and the whole world.

The Great Seal of the United States was designed in 1782 some 3 centuries after Christianity first came to America. The number "3" is Divine, "3" is the Trinity of God, Father, Son and Holy Spirit! Welcome Jesus Christ, Holy Spirit and Our Father to the good old USA!

When the dollar bill was redesigned in 1935 and the Masons thought that their symbol had prevailed, they were totally wrong. You see, "1" is The Father, and He passed judgment "9" together with The Trinity "3" on the wounds "5" inflicted upon His people! The "5" also is a reminder to us of the "5" gifts of correction "Wherefore I am satisfied, for Christ's sake, with infirmities, with insults, with hardships, with persecutions, with distresses. For when I am weak, then I am strong."[86] Masonry is a loser. I urge all Christians to leave it now!

The Great Seal of the United States makes reference to The Eye of our Triune God atop the 13-step pyramid on the reverse of the Seal and does not offend Catholics nor any other Christians because it reminds us of the words of the psalmist "I will fix My eye upon thee...Behold the eye of God is on them that fear Him, and on them that hope in His mercy...He that formeth the eye, doth He not see?"[87]

The Great Seal of the United States as printed on the one dollar bill is broken into two parts, reminding us of the humanity and divinity of Jesus. The first part of "The Great Seal" has 12 letters reminding us of Divine Order and Divine Government. It reminds us of the 12 Apostles and is a constant reminder to read Holy Scripture. The second part "of the United States" has 17 letters which is "1" God, and "7" Spirit and Perfection. In Spirit and Perfection the Government of God will reign in total Spiritual Perfection in the United States of America, and soon.

25

When we examine The Great Seal we see the eagle. Oh how sweet it is to be reminded of the promise and the encouragement "They that hope in the Lord shall renew their strength, they shall take wings as eagles, they shall run and not be weary, they shall walk and not faint!"[88] Praise The Lord, what beauty and strength he bestows upon we His people! To His Babylonian enemies He cautions them "Lift not up thy eyes to riches which thou canst not have, because they shall make themselves wings like those of an eagle, and shall fly towards Heaven."[89] Yes Christians, "thy youth shall be renewed as the eagle's!"[90] Leave the doomed Freemasonry, now!

There are 4 talons in each of the 2 claws. "2" reminds us that "There is Another" and also of the two distinct natures in Christ, Divine and human. "4" is universal and the Will of Jesus Christ prevails in ALL things.

The 32 feathers on one wing and 33 feathers on the other are a reminder of the Divine Trinity thrice stated! "2" is Jesus Christ and "33" is His age at His Crucifixion. Jesus Son of God, came in the flesh, lived among us, died, was buried, rose on the third day from the dead, ascended into Heaven and will come again to judge the living and the dead. Summarized and easily remembered, "Christ has died, Christ is risen, Christ will come again." These 'enlightenments' are symbolized in The Great Seal. Just as God used a donkey to prophesy,[91] so too the designers of The Great Seal were used for His greater glory. God turned their blasphemy to His greater glory.

Perhaps a light hearted note here might be in order. One of my few friends, who happens to be a supporter of the Republican Party, commented "that the 'symbol' of the Democratic Party of Roosevelt, Wallace and Farley is a donkey!" There are may references to donkeys in the bible but there are not too many scriptural references to elephants, the 'symbol' of the Republican Party. The only one I am aware of is in the First book of Maccabees, where the terrorist Antiochus Ephianes used these beasts as weapons in his great army.[92] Deceit and terror marked his reign. Prophetic? Depends how you vote!

The nine tail feathers represent the "9" of judgment which is now stated for the second time. When something in Holy Scriptures is repeated it means that the word of God will be fulfilled, and speedily. "That thou didst see the second time a dream pertaining to the same thing, it is a token of the certainty that the word of God comes to pass, and is fulfilled speedily."[93]

They also remind us of the "9" gifts of the Holy Spirit! There are a variety of gifts from the same Spirit, the same Lord, and the same God, the same

26

Trinity! The gifts of wisdom, knowledge, faith, healing, miracles, prophecy, distinguishing, tongues and interpretations of tongues.[94]

We are also reminded of the gifts of the "9" fruits of the Holy Spirit, "Love, joy, peace, patience, kindness, goodness, faithfulness, gentleness and self-control."[95]

To complete a Trinity of reminders of "9," we are reminded of the "9" spices of Canticles[96] with which we are renewed and invigorated by the word of God.

There are 28 sun burst rays around the 13 stars, Jesus emphasizing that He will come a second time "2" and make all things right (a new beginning). "8" just as He said to Moses, "'Put thy hand into thy bosom.' And when he put his hand into his bosom, he brought it forth leprous as snow. And He said, 'Put back thy hand into thy bosom.' He put it back, and brought it out again, and it was like the other flesh."[97]

There are 14 bright clouds around the sun rays to remind us that "1" God is in control of the "4" universe. "Sing ye to the Lord...Who covered the heaven with clouds...For Thy mercy is above the heavens and Thy truth even unto the clouds...Bless the Lord, O my soul...Who makes the clouds Thy chariot."[98] We will see Him when He comes again "coming upon a cloud with POWER AND MAJESTY,"[99] just as the angels had told the 500 who watched Him ascend in a cloud, "This Jesus Who has been taken up from you into Heaven, shall come in the same way as you have seen Him going up to Heaven."[100]

There are 13 stars in the crest above the eagle.
There are 13 letters in the ribbon "E Pluribus Unum." "Both He Who sanctifies and they who are sanctified, are all from One."[101]
There are 13 bars in the shield.
There are 13 arrows.
There are 13 leaves on the olive branch.
There are 13 original states of significant importance.
There are 13 granite stones!
There are 13 letters "Annuit Coeptis," A new beginning. Born Again.

"8" times the number "13" is stated in The Great Seal. When the founding fathers came to America they came to a "new world" for a new beginning. "8" is the number for a "new beginning." and just as eight people boarded Noah's ark for the "new world," so too The Great Seal reminds all of professed Christendom of the promise of God to lead us into "a land of

27

milk and honey!" "8" times the Great Seal reminds us of "1", "God The Father" and the "3" of the Divine Trinity of The Father, Jesus Christ The Messiah and The Holy Spirit. The significance of the victory by God the Creator is already foretold and therefore guaranteed.

There are "4" written captions in Latin and again God is reminding us of His Divine promise. 12 times the number "3" has been recalled in The Great Seal. "12" is Divine order. "12" is Government. "12" is Maturity or fulfillment. God The Creator of all things is reminding us of His Divine Government, His Divine Order, His Divine Maturity.

"E Pluribus Unum" reminds us of the Morning Star, "From many, one." "MDCCLXXVI," means "1776" and signifies that 1 God The Father in the "7" Spirit of "7" Perfection, will give "6" man all that was promised. "He Who has begun a good work in you (America) will bring it to perfection until the day of Christ Jesus."[102] The "9" Latin letters signifying Holy Judgment for a 3rd time reminds us forcefully of what is to come. What is the significance of "76?" In the Bible, "angels, angel or angel's" are mentioned over 300 times, "76" times in the Book of Revelation, The Apocalypse. The choirs of angels are sent to execute God's judgment on earth. Look at what the 3 angels of the Apocalypse have to say.

The first angel says, "Fear God, and give Him honor, FOR THE HOUR OF HIS JUDGMENT HAS COME; and worship Him Who made the Heaven and the earth, the sea and the fountain of waters."[103]

The second angel says, "She has fallen, Babylon the great, who of the wine of the wrath of her immorality has given all the nations to drink."[104]

The third angel says, "If anyone worships the beast and its image and receives a mark upon his forehead or upon his hand, he also shall drink of the wine of the wrath of God, which is poured unmixed into the cup of His wrath; and he shall be tormented with fire and brimstone in the sight of the holy angels and in the sight of the Lamb. And the smoke of their torments goes up for ever and ever; and they rest neither day nor night, they who have worshipped the beast and its image, and anyone who receives the mark of its name."[105]

"Annuit Coeptis," which translated means "New Beginning," reminds Catholics and all other Christians that God keeps His word.

"Novus Ordo Seclorum" or "New World Order" is a reminder to all Catholics and the rest of Christianity of the fulfillment which will shortly

28

take place "I saw a new heaven and a new earth. For the first heaven and the first earth passed away, and the sea is no more. And I saw the holy city, New Jerusalem, coming down out of Heaven from God."[106] The original 'world order' given by God in the Garden of Eden will be restored. The New World Order given by the devil and propagated by the modern Babylonian leaders is on it's way to destruction and damnation.

In summary there are 24 articles in The Great Seal which we have just recalled. That is "2" times "12" which reminds us that Jesus is coming a second time and His Government will prevail, and He is coming soon! All these articles Glorify God, and in His Glory America came to be. It is in this Glory that we Catholics and all of professed Christendom recall for Christ and His Kingdom that the flag of the USA is called after Jesus Christ and the Ancient of Days, "Old Glory!"

Since the hour of judgement has come, it is time to get away from the evil Babylonian system of voodoo in which we are living and renew our fidelity to Jesus. As we look to the emblems on the US dollar bill, let us be constantly reminded of Jesus and look for Him to renew the face of the earth

CHAPTER 5

THE MONEY SYSTEM

"She has fallen, Babylon the great, who of the wine of the wrath of her immorality has given all the nations to drink."[104]

Who or what is Babylon?

In Genesis, Chapter 10, we learn that Noah's sons were Shem, Ham and Japheth; Ham fathered Cush, Mizraim, Put and Canaan. Cush fathered Nimrod who became the world's first great conqueror. Nimrod founded Babel and "the beginning of his kingdom was Babel (Babylon), and Arach (Erech), and Achad (Accad), and Chalanne (Calneh) in the land of Sennar (Shinar)."[107] The land of Shinar is in Iraq and Babylon is about 55 miles south-west of modern Baghdad.

"The earth was of the one tongue, and of the same speech...and when they moved from the east, they found a plain in the land of Shinar, and dwelt in it. And each one said to his neighbor, 'Come, let us make brick, and bake them with fire.' And they had brick instead of stones, and slime instead of mortar. And they said, 'Come, let us make a city and a tower, the top whereof may reach to heaven; and let us make our name famous...And the Lord came down to see the city and the tower...and He said...it is one people and all have one tongue. And they have begun to do this, neither will they leave off from their designs, till they accomplish them in deed...let Us...confound their tongue, that they may not understand one another's speech'...therefore the name thereof was called Babel, because there the language of the whole earth was confounded; and from thence the Lord scattered them abroad upon the face of all the countries."[108]

Babylon was a wealthy kingdom, the kings of which, trusting in their own power and might, silver and gold, were cruel and merciless in the pursuit of that power and money. We are told in Daniel, chapter 3, that when King Nabuchadnezzar, the direct lineage of Nimrod, had subdued the towns, provinces and all the inhabitants of the then known world, from India to Ethiopia, he had a golden statue made and commanded his magistrates, governors, petty tyrants, counsellors, treasurers, judges, lawyers, all the provincial authorities, all the people, nations and languages, to prostrate themselves and worship his statue.

The king boasted "Is not this the great Babylon, which I have built to be the seat of the kingdom, by the strength of my power, and in the glory of my excellence?"[109] It was one of the wonders of the ancient world.

"Who or what is Babylon?" It's name is the symbol for boasting of human achievements and giving credit to oneself rather than to God. It symbolizes arrogance, both human and satanic. It symbolizes that which is false, made of clay and slime. We shall see that our modern governments and money systems are built on deceit and oppression, clay and slime.

Babylon was destroyed by the Medes in 539 BC in fulfillment of the prophecy of Isaiah "I will visit the evils of the world, and against the wicked for their iniquity, and I will make the pride of infidels to cease, and will bring down the arrogancy of the mighty...every man shall return to his own people, and every one shall flee to his own land...Behold I shall stir up the Medes against them...It shall no more be inhabited forever."[110] (We see the destruction of this 'arrogancy of the mighty' today, presidents and kings abdicating, high officials indited and jailed, tycoons incarcerated, all at an increase in numbers and speed).

The Babylonians were further prophesied against by Isaiah and it applies to this present day, "for thou shalt no more be called the lady of kingdoms...thou hast shewn no mercy to them (the Lord's people), upon the ancient thou hast laid thy yoke exceeding heavy ...These two things shall come upon thee suddenly in one day, barrenness and widowhood."[111] (The rulers barren of power, the manipulators widowed from their wealth).

We shall see a little later that oppressive taxes and runaway inflation are an unbearable yoke which today's rulers impose on the people, the same rulers who 'forecast' economic events with consistent inaccuracy. "Flee from the midst of Babylon...be not silent upon her iniquity, for it is the time of revenge from the Lord...Babylon hath been a golden cup in the hand of the Lord, that made all the earth drunk, the nations have drunk of her wine, and therefore they have staggered...Upon the walls of Babylon set up the standard...prepare the ambushes...O thou that dwellest upon many waters, rich in treasures, thy end is come for thy entire destruction."[112]

"Raise the standard throughout the world, sound the trumpet among the nations! Consecrate nations to make war on her; summon kingdoms against her!"[113] Just as the United Nations in the resolutions of 1990 consecrated themselves to make war on Babylon (Iraq), and just as the Lord has influenced the hearts of the rulers to execute His purpose, so too He has ordained that the Babylonian money system installed by the world will collapse. This system is already in chaos and is crumbling further daily. The three great money centers of the world today are London, New York and Tokyo. As international disruptions take place, the financial gamblers of the world seek safe refuge in the US Dollar, not the British Pound or the Japanese Yen but the US Dollar which they know is already bankrupt! This has a particular meaning which we will see shortly.

This situation has been carefully planned by the money powers of the world. The position in the USA is this. The Western countries' central banks hold $350 billion in US dollars and US Treasury notes. The US reserve has $100 billion in gold reserves plus $40 billion in other Western countries' financial instruments. The US has $140 billion and owes $350 billion. The US is broke by any legitimate accounting standard. Each month the trade deficit runs between $5 billion and $12 billion depending on the lies told about the statistics. Yet in time of financial crisis, the world has been influenced to seek shelter in the USA which they know is sinking further and further into debt. How pitiful to think that smart people have been so deceived (or manipulated).

Man's government, fueled by ego and greed, has resulted in spiraling costs, inflation, famine, homelessness and destitution. Today some countries have inflation rates in excess of 10,000% per year. In these cases the wage earners have to be paid twice a day in an attempt to buy food with current decreasing (money) 'script.' Why is the economic standard so out of control in the world? The answer is very simple, man has rejected God and established his modern Babylonian standard. God gave us an economic standard with which to work...gold and silver...man rejected it.

How did this out of hand satanical system of voodoo get started? Let us look at what God gave us and see how man has corrupted it.

God gave us gold. It is the first precious metal mentioned in the Old Testament, in the first book, Genesis 2:11, and in the first book of the New Testament, Matthew 2:11. It is also the last mentioned precious metal in the Bible, in Revelation 21:21. In Genesis we are told that there is gold in the land of Havilah, and "the gold of that land is good."[114] It is the first earthly gift that Jesus received, and finally the saints will walk on it, as the streets of the New Jerusalem are of pure gold.

Gold was a sign of riches, "(Abraham) was very rich in possession of gold and silver."[115] Gold and silver were measured in shekels and when Abraham was buying the field he paid for it with "four hundred shekels of silver according to current money."[116] In Exodus we are introduced to the sanctuary shekel.[117] God is an exact 'detailst' and in His word He gives us guidelines on what the weights should be. The shekel must be 20 gerah. Twenty shekels, twenty five shekels and fifteen shekels must weigh one mina.[118] In order to correlate these to our modern weights, one mina = 1.50 lbs. God wants us to use His standard, His measurements, His ways, so that we would have accuracy and no confusion. He made the world and all in it. He made all of us.

In Old Testament times, the determination of just weights and balances was not an easy matter and the dishonest had two weights, a lesser and a greater, one for buying and a different one for selling. God tells us "Do not any unjust thing in judgment, in rule, in weight or in measure. Let the balance be just and the weights equal."[119] He warns us "Hear this you that crush the poor and make the needy of the land to fail, saying...'we can lessen the measure and increase the shekel and may convey in deceitful balances, that we may possess the needy for money and the poor for a pair of shoes and may sell (them) the refuse of corn...The Lord hath sworn against the pride of Jacob, 'Surely I will never forget all their works.'"[120]

Man minted coins as a convenient method of carrying gold and silver, and this was good. The coins were measured by size, weight and by metal, thus establishing values. The first record of coins is in the seventh century BC by the Lydians. The Persians conquered the Lydians and they liked the idea of the coins and promptly minted their own, and so this good idea spread to the Greeks, the Babylonians and the Romans. These rulers liked the idea of having their image stamped on the obverse of the coin and the symbol of their power on the reverse...humble men they were not, and in the mold of Nabuchadnezzar! The idea has not lost any of it's luster to this very day, and in the USA the power on the currencies states "In God We Trust"...but the God of Revelation is not allowed in school, or in work, or in government or public places...this is a criminal offence! More on this later.

When coins were first minted, they had a specific value. For example, a one ounce silver coin contained one ounce of pure silver. Using the legitimate reason that in order to make the coin stronger and more durable, alloys were added. As the silver was spent and the government needed more money, the silver was replaced by an alloy (leaven) and, as at present, dross has replaced our silver! Saint Paul tells us "Do you not know that a little leaven leavens the whole lump?"[121] The leaven was unpretentious in the beginning but was destined for enormous growth.

Coins gave way to paper money for further convenience. The paper money

33

was backed by gold and silver in the national vaults and as the rulers had the key to the national vaults, the key to the printing presses for the printing of money, they had the source of 'money' to satisfy their egos. Paper money was printed against the deposits of gold and silver which were supposed to have been issued under just balances. The paper money was in essence a cheque, drawn on a sovereign government, promising to pay that value in gold or silver.

Let us take a very simple example of how the system should work. Suppose USA Sam gave a dollar to London Bull in payment for goods, in which Bull expected to be paid an ounce of gold when he cashed in his dollar. As long as the US government was honest and had as many ounces in its vaults as it had for the dollars printed, the system worked, the US government could be trusted and everyone fared very well. Suppose however, that the government printed twice as many dollars as it had gold and it now took two dollars to buy that one ounce, when Bull went to cash in his dollar he was cheated. By fraudulently tampering with the scales, the US government adjusted the weights to suit its own purpose. This dishonesty gave rise to inflation among other things.

That is exactly what happened. We started off trading with these precious metals. Then as the governors, driven by their greedy desire for power and monopoly, spent the gold and silver for weapons of war, and having taxed the people excessively, they had to look elsewhere for money to satisfy their cravings. They borrowed from a people yet to be born, and saddled them with crushing taxation long before they are weaned. This was all part of a pre-ordained plot on the part of world manipulators.

The total known gold reserves in the world, both mined and unmined would only form a cube of about 30 yards high (about 135,000 tons)! Realizing this, the 'super powers' of the world decided since they had plenty of paper and ink but not sufficient gold they would scrap God's system and print the financial 'super-lie' of all time, "the floating currency". This is a method in which a country reports its statistics each period and based on the relative strength for that period, the international debts are paid and currencies exchanged.

The foundation for our money system was abolished. One normally thinks of a foundation as ROCK solid. We were given a "floating currency", a "floating" foundation. Who ever built a foundation on water? Yet this is exactly what has happened! The whole lump was leavened! The floating currencies is a lie, is voodoo and is a product of confusion (fusion is from God, confusion is from the snake, Satan). Within the world currencies, the

European Monetary System monitors the currencies of its member states within "the snake system." The Common Market governments' central bankers nod their heads with feigned wisdom and understanding and "adjust within the snake." They have already professed Satan!

Born in an era of political subterfuge, bred in a climate of economic unrestraint, fueled by insatiable egos, the world was plunged into the present state of disunity, uncertainty and confusion. The governments of the world have 'drunk deep of the wine of their prostitution', and are now bankrupt through their own planned mismanagement. They issue a series of 'indices' and figures each month which supposedly indicate the strength of their country's economy. The indices are deviously used and are a liar's ideal tool for creating a 'false balance'. When the index is made public, and misstated, then at some time in the future there has to be an 'adjustment' or a 'correction of previously released figures.' Satanism at its most financial cunning.

Why have we so many homeless? Why has the budget increased 500% more than the 'poor' wage? Why has the hidden tax of state and county increased 600% in the same 20 year period? "When all the prisoners in a country are crushed underfoot, when human rights are overridden in defiance of the Most High, when someone is cheated of justice, does not the Lord see it?"[122] The Lord will not reject anyone for ever.

We watch the every day fluctuation in the value of the dollar relative to other currencies and the precious metals; we watch the government's mismanagement of the economy and its capricious handling of the dollar printing presses. We are told that gold is up or silver is down; this is rubbish, the value of gold and silver is not changing, it is the value of paper money...'the floating currency.' Man's ego and greed plus his innate belief in his own invincibility are fueling the economy to higher numbers, the stock markets to renewed cockiness and his arrogance to acceptance of the abnormal and the rejection of truth.

The USA was the prime mover in abandoning God's standard and thus degrading society. In 1971 the US had its first trade deficit in almost 30 years. These deficits continued for five months from March through July. In August the French demanded payment of some $300 million US dollars for gold, followed by the Japanese with $1.2 billion, and the English decided that it was time to exchange $3 billion for gold. America could not pay so the then President Nixon and Treasurer Secretary Connoly abandoned the gold standard and established the 'floating currencies.' (Nixon later was forced to resign, politically bankrupt, Connoly declared bankruptcy).

The rush was on, the 'rock' was abandoned, the 'float' was born and Babylon, that system of confusion, was well on its way to total control of the world monetary system. How have the American people benefitted? The US budget in 1971 was $190 billion, and by 1992 it was $1.5 trillion, or $1,500 billion (about a 760% increase)!

Compare the US statistics since the end of the gold standard:

	1971	1992	Increase
Population (millions)	208	249	20%
GNP (trillions=T$)	$1.2	$ 4.9	308%
Budget.[a] (T$)	$ .19	$ 1.5	760%
Debt.[b] (T$)	$ .52	$ 3.46	565%
Annual interest on Debt[c] (T$)	$ .03	$ .85	
Per person share of National Debt	$2,500	$14,000	460%
Per family share of National Debt[d]	$7,900	$43,000	
Minimum Wage	$1.60	$ 4.25	165%
Silver per ounce	$1.50	$ 3.59	
Gold per ounce	$35	$359	
Ratio silver/gold (11 Feb '91)	23:1	100:1	

[a]   Office of Management of the Budget.
[b]   US Bureau of Debt.
[c] The US Dept. of Treasury reports that this is the total debt over time is divided into two areas, Marketable and Non-Marketable (e.g. US Savings Bonds). The above amount excludes the Non-Marketable interest in the amount of T$1.85.
[d] Debt plus the total interest obligations over time now exceeds T$5.4 which is about $22,000/person or $58,000/family.

These are all statistics, so what is the real meaning and what are we to do with them?

One answer is that the governors are mismanaging the affairs of the citizens at a rate 300 times faster than the population growth; burdening the people with a debt 500 times greater than when they started; increasing their own living standards while seemingly increasing the minimum wage but in actual fact reducing the 'poor' to dispossession and slavery.

None of us has the ability to predict the future. There is only One who can and He asks us to walk in His word by faith. He gave us gold and silver as the basis for our currency and history records that whenever man has abandoned His Story and proceeded without Him, confusion has reigned. Today the world of economics is in confusion, the governments are bankrupt, financially and morally. Some analysts say they are blindly searching for the way out; I seriously doubt it. If they were they would return to God's way, the only way, the real basis of money, gold and silver. "How is the faithful city, that was full of judgment, become a harlot?...Thy silver is turned into dross...Thy princes are faithless, companions of thieves, they all love bribes, they run after rewards...I will comfort Myself over My adversaries, and I will be revenged of My enemies. And I will turn My hand to thee, and I will purge away ALL thy dross, and I will take away ALL thy tin (alloy). And I will restore your judges as they were before...After this thou shalt be called the city of the just, a faithful city."[123]

The ROCK solid has been disregarded in favor of dross. Prudence has been abandoned in favor of greed. Truth has been disregarded in favor of innuendo. In 1920 George B. Shaw wrote, "You have to choose between trusting to the natural stability of gold and the honesty and intelligence of members of the government, I advise you as long as the capitalist system lasts, to vote for gold." Some seventy years later another George B. was to be heard saying "Read my lips!" This George B. is so human. Today the "king makers" package their hand picked politicians for media presentation so as to make them look perfect. After they are finished 'packaging' the poor subjects act dumb. Not so with this George B., he says what is on his mind...some of the time!

Jesus warned us "Every plant that My Heavenly Father has not planted will be rooted up...They are blind guides of blind men. But if a blind man guide a blind man, both will fall into a pit"[124] and again "Take heed; beware of the leaven of the Pharisees and of the leaven of Herod!"[125]

How much do the leaders know and where are they leading? Since the handing over of our money system to the foreign powers who own the Federal Reserve System, it takes $9 today to purchase the same amount of goods $1 bought in 1914, a 900% increase. We have been sold into slavery by our crooked politicians who are wolves in sheep's clothing. These pawns of the "invisible government by the money power" are knowingly pillaging the citizenry in exchange for temporal power. But then a country gets the government it deserves.

These faithless princes and bribe-laden companions of thieves are being purged from our society more and more. From the highest political office to the false board of directors, the Lord's hand has turned to punish them.

CHAPTER 6

THE GOVERNMENT

Let us understand how the government of man came about.

God created all things. He created the earth and the fullness thereof, the world and all it contains belong to Him; He owns the cattle on a thousand hills, He knows when a sparrow falls to the ground. He knows every hair on our heads and every thought in our hearts. He created man and gave him care of the earth. In His great mercy He has told man how to govern himself, but man has not listened. He gave us Himself as our Leader "I shall fix My home among you and never reject you. I shall live among you; I shall be your God, and you shall be My people."[126] But man rejected Him and demanded an earthly king. In anticipation of this God said "If, having reached the country given by the Lord your God and having taken possession of it and, while living there you think, 'I should like to appoint a king to rule me like surrounding nations,' the king whom you appoint to rule...once seated on his royal throne, and for his own use, he must write a copy of this Law on a scroll, at the dictation of the Levitical priests. It must never leave him, and he must read it every day of his life and learn to fear The Lord his God by keeping all the words of this Law and observing these rules, so that he will not think himself superior to his brothers."[127]

Man did demand a king, who rejected the Law of God, as God foretold, "This is what the king who is to rule over you will do. He will take your sons and direct them to his chariotry and cavalry, and they will run in front of his chariot...he will make them plough his fields and gather in his harvest, and make his weapons of war and gear for his chariot. He will take your daughters as perfumers, cooks and bakers. He will take the best of your fields, your vineyards and your olive groves and give them to his officials. He will tithe your crops and vineyards to provide for his courtiers and his officials. He will take the best of your servants, men and women, of your oxen and donkeys and make them work for him. He will tithe your flocks and you yourselves will become his slaves. When that day comes, you will cry aloud because of the king you have chosen for yourselves, but on that day the Lord will not hear you."[128]

That is an accurate prophecy of today's governments made some 4,000 years ago. Do not the governments of the world take our youth and put them into the service? Today do not the governments of the world have as the single largest item of expenditure in their budget "weapons of war?" As stated previously "One answer is that the Government is mismanaging the affairs of the citizens at a rate 300 times greater than the population growth; burdening the people with a debt 500 times greater than when they started." Do we not see today the courtiers and officials taking the peoples taxes to provide for their own personal gain? Do we not see overcharging of contracts to provide for bribery and stealing? Who owns the choicest property? Do we not see officials on the inside 'in the know' privately acquire property which they will sell to the Government for exorbitant profits, at the expense of the taxpayers?

Does not the major portion of the world's income go in payment of taxes, both direct and indirect? How many days each week must the ordinary working person, the cook, baker, mechanic, soldier, accountant, clerk, farmer, cashier and the average wage earner have to work for the payment of their taxes before they earn a penny for themselves? "Why have we so many homeless? Why has the budget increased 500% more than the 'poor' wage? Why has the hidden tax of state and county increased 600%?"

The modern day governments started innocently enough and with well meaning plans. For example, the US Constitution decentralized powers with the Federal Government controlling the executive, legislative, judicial and state governments. Business, finance, labor, education and charity were outside the direct control of the Federal Government. Since that time all of the above has come under the authority and control and power of the Federal Government. How did that happen? The government had to borrow money to pay for its bungling inefficiencies, ego mania, ridiculous war machines, and creeping socialism to gain absolute control and power over the citizens. It was influenced by the Freemasonry 'beast like a leopard,' working in the shadows to subvert society and bring on the disintegration of person, family, community, and finally the state. When the taxes were not enough to pay for its appetite, the government set about encouraging expansion of business and education through subsidies...and whatever it subsidizes it must regulate. The Supreme Court has ruled that absolute power over the people was and is in the absolute control of the Federal Government. Every part of an American's life is now numbered and legislated from birth to burial; one cannot even get married before God without first getting permission (license) from the local government and meeting all its requirements. Within two years of birth a child is given a number. This is its "social security number" which is used in the computers to identify and trace all of the individual's activities for the rest of it's life.

39

A brief look at taxation will show us to where the final injustice leads.

We read in Nehemiah (this was about 450 BC) "We have had to borrow money on our fields and on our vineyards to pay the royal tax...we shall have to sell our sons and daughters into slavery; some of our daughters have been sold into slavery already. We can do nothing about it, since our fields and vineyards now belong to others."[129] We read of Nehemiah vindicating his own administration for not levying the governor's subsistence allowance; "whereas the former governors, my predecessors, had been a burden on the people, from whom they took forty silver shekels a day for food and wine, while their attendants oppressed the people too."[130] 40 silver shekels weighed about 16 ounces, and at today's current commercial rate of about $4, this is $64. How many people today do we know who have had to mortgage their property, their farms, their buildings and their possessions just to pay the tax? How many people do you know who have had to hand their property over to the state just because they could not pay the tax? Is it not true that every official entity which in any way can claim a public status charges taxes? National, state, county, city, school district, hospital district, water, road, bridge, airport etc. Is it not true then, that a tax is charged on almost everything we buy with the money that is left after we pay tax on what we earn, and that the people are made to collect the taxes for the king?

Look at how a group of governments can move together to control masses of people through international taxation. After the Treaty of Rome on 25 March 1958, the Common Market was born. Originally there were 6 members, Italy, Germany, France, Belgium, Luxembourg and The Netherlands (also called Holland). In 1962 it became known as The European Economic Community, the EEC. Ireland, Denmark and Britain joined in January 1973, followed by Greece in January 1981 and finally by Portugal and Spain in January 1986, a total of 12 members. This world order has imposed a system of taxation which is called "Value Added Tax" or simply "VAT." Under this program a tax is added to every piece of material that is manufactured and is taxed progressively as manufacturing is added by different companies until finally the ultimate consumer pays all. VAT is charged and paid progressively by the manufacturers, wholesalers and retailers who are simultaneously the tax payer and the tax collector for the government! The average VAT rate is 22%. The EEC citizens in some countries pay as high as 85% total direct and indirect taxes. Freedom or slavery?

Merchandise itself does not cost that much, it is the tax that costs. "Give up your violence and plundering, do what is right and just, stop crushing

My people with taxation - declares the Lord God."[131] And yet the governments of the world continue to mismanage and charge ever increasing taxes and add the yoke of oppression and slavery to the wage earner. The words of the prophet Haggai say "The wage earner gets his wages only to put them in a bag with a hole in it."[132] Note the words 'wage earner,' not the industrialist or the rulers who have a different system for reporting 'income,' usually a trust or foundation; no, it is the 'wage earner'. Yet God told Moses "You will not be unjust in administering justice as regards measures of length, weight or capacity."[133] He warns us "A false balance is an abomination to the Lord."[134] Make no mistake about it, God has in the past, is now and will again in the near future correct and rebuke those who have inflicted these injustices, "All the nations have drunk deep of the wine of her prostitution; every king on the earth has prostituted himself with her, and every merchant grown rich through her debauchery...She must be paid double the amount she exacted. She is to have a doubly strong cup of her own mixture."[135] And so the excessive taxes, the provided legal tax loopholes for the merchant and the officials, have already earned the retribution of The Almighty.

Even with the plundering of the citizenry, the Government still cannot pay it's way so it has had to borrow from the people and the banks. It has issued bonds and treasury bills and other sorts of promissory notes. The Government encouraged the banks to lend to developing businesses and then to developing countries. "The nations have fallen into the trap they made, their feet caught in the snare they laid."[136] Let us look at four major historical US banking events which are central to the issue today.

FIRST was the panic bank run in 1907 planned by J. Pierpont Morgan, which saw the end of a number of his rival banks and the establishment of his associates' banks in a position of preeminence within the American banking system.

SECOND was the establishment of a central bank called the Federal Reserve System as a result of the 1907 run...the prime movers for the central bank were Morgan and his associates. When the Federal Reserve Act was rushed through Congress just before the Christmas recess on 22 December 1913, the American people had unwittingly handed over control of their financial destiny to the Chairman of the Federal Reserve Board, who was and is in the control or at the mercy of the international lenders. These lenders have all the central banks of the other countries in a similar position. Congressman Lindberg Sr. said after the vote, "This act establishes the most gigantic trust on earth...When the President signs this act THE INVISIBLE GOVERNMENT BY THE MONEY POWER, proven

41

to exist by the Money Trust investigation, will be legalized...This new law will create inflation whenever the trusts want inflation..."[137] The 'Fed' controls the printing press or money supply, it sets and controls interest rates, it has never been audited, and Congress has no authority over it. It creates inflation and it creates deflation to it's own end and purpose. The unwitting American public who deem themselves to be "informed" believe that the Federal Reserve is a part of their Government. The Federal Reserve is no more a branch of the Government than Federal Express or Federal Paper Hangers, Inc. Since it's formation, the federal debt has risen from $1 billion to $5.4 trillion ($5,400 billion) including accumulated interest payments! "We the people" of America, every man, woman and child, each owe $22,000 to the "invisible government" in payment of the national debt. Notice the following dangerous trend:

1924 Federal Reserve began open market operations.
1933 Legal tender laws were permanently enacted.
1934 FDR prohibits private ownership of gold.
1945 Gold reserves for Federal Reserve Notes and Deposits decreased from 35% to 25%
1962 Last year in which 90% circulating silver coins were minted by the Government.
1968 Last 25% of gold reserves for Federal Reserve Notes and Deposits removed.
1971 Nixon ends international redeemability of Federal Reserve Note.

THIRD. In addition to it's grip on the banks, the 'Fed' has been handed the reins of total control of the S&Ls. The failed FSLIC is now under FDIC control. The rescue plan put forward by President Bush promised to cost the taxpayers $120 billion, his estimate in 1989. It is now costing the taxpayers $500 billion. As more banks fail at unprecedented rates, select banks are taking over the failed banks at the expense of the taxpayer and to the enhancement of the internationalists, THE INVISIBLE GOVERNMENT BY THE MONEY POWER! The government, having encouraged international lending, now finds many banks in trouble and has devised some rather interesting solutions.

For example, the US banks are owed $240 billion by the failing Latin American countries. The Latin debt is selling on the open market for 33 cents on the dollar, which in effect says that the $240 billion is only worth $80 billion. The Bush-Baker-Brady plan of rescue calls for a 20% forgiveness of the Latin debt, thus reducing it to $192 billion and that amount would be guaranteed by the US Government, the International Monetary Fund and the World Bank. This is a sweet deal for the banks

42

which now get a 20% tax write-off, get a bad-debt instrument presently worth only $80 billion replaced by a government backed $192 billion bond, thanks to the oppressed taxpayers. The 'Fed' is rubbing its greedy big hands while the Government is in effect nationalizing the banks for the final and ultimate hand-over of the control of the money to "invisible government," Freemasonry.

Having shipped the jobs of the Americans abroad, financed by the American banks, subsidized by the Government, refinanced by the unsuspecting taxpayers ("My people perish for lack of knowledge"[138]) the prophecy is fulfilled, "Into the land of distress and anguish, of lioness and roaring lion, of viper and flying dragon, they bear their riches on donkeys' backs, their treasures on camels' humps (747's) to a nation that cannot help..."[139] Into the land of Freemasonry, with its Egyptian symbols and voodoo, the jobs and equity have been shipped. All the mechanics will have been handed over to the international lenders who have only one small detail to add before they make the borrower the ultimate slave. The government has requested permission to allow them accept credit cards in payment of income and other taxes.

"Woe to those who enact unjust decrees, who compose oppressive legislation to deny justice to the weak and to cheat the humblest of My people of fair judgment, to make widows their prey and to rob the orphan. What will you do on the day of judgment, when disaster comes from far away? To whom will you run for help and where will you leave your riches, to avoid squatting among the captives or falling among the slain?"[140] How then will the US leaders respond to this challenge? Are they in the power of the demons who use the governments and rulers of this world as their tools? "We do talk of wisdom, not...a philosophy of this age or of the rulers of this age, who will not last long now."[141]

FOURTH. The American people, no different from those of the rest of the world, have been sheepishly led into the world of false money via the medium of the credit card. As cash is depleted and the money supply is reduced, the Government will accept (allow!) payment of taxes by credit card. When this happens the Government will finally "have power over the treasures of gold and of silver and all the precious things."[142] The government is under the control of the Federal Reserve, which is controlled by the "3 bankers." The people have pledged their security to the banks and are paying interest and usury at slaves' rates.

Let us be clear about the definitions of interest and usury. Interest is a charge on a loan, usually a percentage of the amount borrowed. Usury is

43

the act or practice of lending money at excessive interest rates; an exorbitant OR illegal rate of interest.

The Word of God teaches us a lot about these terms and in fact lays down absolute laws for the use of money.

"If you lend money to My people, to the poor among you, you are not to act as a creditor to him; you shall not charge him interest...And it shall come about that when he calls upon Me, I shall hear him, for I am gracious."[143] "Now in case a countryman of yours becomes poor and his means with regard to you falter, then you are to sustain him, like a stranger or sojourner, that he may live with you. Do not take usurious interest from him, but revere your God, that your countryman may live with you. You shall not give him your silver at interest, nor your food for gain."[144] "You shall not charge interest to your countrymen; interest on money, food, or anything that may be loaned at interest. You may charge interest to a foreigner, but to your countryman you shall not charge interest."[145] "You are exacting usury, each from his brother!... now you would even sell your brothers...Please let us leave off this usury...give back to them this very day their fields, their vineyards, their olive groves, and their houses, also the hundredth part of the money and of the grain, the new wine, and all the oil that you are exacting from them."[146]"He who increases his wealth by interest and usury, gathers it for him who is gracious to the poor."[147]

Most people using credit cards are paying only a percentage of the balance due on the card each month. They cannot afford the goods which were purchased in the first place, but mostly because of pride they buy. The users of the card fall prey to the usurious interest charges of the card companies, whose rates are an excessive 18% per year and even higher. The companies operate from those states whose laws permit usury. Saint Paul teaches us that "As long as the enthusiasm is there, the basis on which it is acceptable is what someone has, not what someone does not have."[148] We should trade on the basis of what we have, not what we do not have, and so we are in keeping with the words "I have neither lent, nor have men lent money to me."[149]

Many people in the world today are living the plastic cashless life. They shop at a store or restaurant based on the credit card signs on the door. Soon, vending machines, road and bridge tolls and any place where money is exchanged will be operated with plastic cards. With the advent of the banks being nationalized and under the control of the "invisible government" of Freemasonry, the last detail to be put in place is to demand that all wages be deposited directly into these banks, which will automatically take out the interest and taxes owed them for the National Debt, replace the credit card (from the Latin word credere, to believe) with a debit card (from the Latin word debere, to owe) and all merchants and citizenry will transact all their money affairs through the 'lenders.' Total control over what is bought and where it is to be bought will be exacted on the citizens of the world. There will be total hardship. The people owe with no belief and pay with no relief. "The rich rules over the poor, and the borrower becomes the lender's slave."[150] The majority of card users are now slaves.

The numbers assigned to our children at birth, social security numbers, will become the number through which this central bank will operate, and it will have done the same thing with the rest of the world. The numbers will become our marks for getting jobs and buying food and other essentials. 'The lender,' which is "the invisible government" of Freemasonry, will exact cruel and harsh terms on the people of the world. It will dictate the price of everything without exception, "A day's wages for a quart of corn, and a day's wages for three quarts of barley, but do not tamper with the oil or the wine."[151] The poor will again be oppressed still further but not the rulers.

Through the largest computer the world has ever seen, the one called "The Beast" in the basement of the European Parliament Headquarters in Brussels, Belgium, the "invisible government" will control every person, every job, every movement, every piece of news media, because it has descended the world into absolute slavery. At the present time the governments of the world are already serving its wishes. Through its citizens' SS number, medical and dental records are compiled, the ultimate in identification. Through its SS number school grades are logged, every aptitude, religious affiliations, club attendance, bars and restaurants frequented. It will record every purchase made, be it at the department store or the grocery store even down to the brand of toilet paper, how the purchases were paid, by credit card or check. It will document the amount of cash taken from the account in any given period, donations made and to whom. All travel will be monitored, what journeys were made by air, by boat, by car (some states now require an odometer reading before they will issue a car permit for the new license year). It will have a record of your place of work, and through the company ID number, all associates and friends; to whom you talk, how often and for how long. The combination of the credit card and the SS number is deadly. Anyone who does not wear his beastly number can neither buy or sell.

Yes, "the New World...the land of the free" has been handed over free to the New World Order! Those believing in the false money are headed for the big crash. The final countdown is on, the Babylonian system of money is collapsing, the world is headed for the final confrontation, and the moral decadence which is an insult to God is putting the hooks deeper and deeper into the jaws of those headed for Armageddon, both particularly and universally. "Calmly I await the day of anguish which is dawning on the people now attacking us."[152]

The "invisible government," through it's leader, will bring the world into the final phase of the great tribulation. In the meantime, be aware of world leaders clamoring for "The New World Order" on the pretext of world peace. We will not know Antichrist's identity for some time because for the time being he is hiding behind "the invisible government of money power." He will come to power and later will be known as that man of iniquity. Just as the evil systems of Satan have come deceptively upon the world through Freemasonry, Communism, the false church and false christ, so too the Antichrist will come quietly into the world and will have worked his way up the ranks of his 'profession.' He will be skilful and devious. He will know man's government, but not God's government.

He is the Antichrist, the beast to whom the devil has "handed over...his own power, throne and his immense authority."[153] "Children, this is the final hour; you have heard that the Antichrist is coming, and now many antichrists have already come; from this we know that it is the final hour."[154] All of the antichrists will hand over their authority to and band together under the Antichrist for the final great conflict.

"Watch yourselves, or your hearts will be coarsened by debauchery and drunkenness and the cares of life, and that day will come upon you unexpectedly, like a trap. For it will come down on all those living on the face of the earth. Stay awake, praying at all times for the strength to survive all that is going to happen, and to hold your ground before the Son of man."[155] If you are not asleep and you decide now to break free like a gazelle from the trap of the fowler and come out of Babylon, there is "a tent to give shade by day from the heat, refuge and shelter from the storm and rain,"[156] and we shall see this in Chapter 10.

CHAPTER 7

COMMUNISM AND FREEMASONRY

"Behold I do new things, and now they shall spring forth."[157] "And it shall come to pass after this that I will pour out My Spirit upon all flesh, and your sons and daughters shall prophesy, your old men dream dreams, and your young people see visions."[158] Mary, the Mother of Jesus and Our Blessed Mother has been appearing publicly in many places to many people in the last 200 years. "I have spoken by the prophets and I have multiplied visions, and I have used similitude by the ministry of the prophets."[159] In recent years, she has revealed by means of "interior locutions" to Father Stefano Gobbi, that among other things she is the Prophetess to the world. God has told us He was going to do something new in our day, and yet there are some who do not and will not believe...at present.

The appearances of Our Lady at Lourdes, La Salette, Knock, Fatima, Caracas, Akita, Medugorje and Africa are well known and witnessed. Although some have not as yet been verified by the Church, the undeniable fact is that the Blessed Virgin Mary has appeared and is appearing and has been physically embraced by some of the visionaries.

Our Lady appeared to three young children in Fatima and they described her as a "woman clothed in the sun."[160] She told them on 13 May 1917 she would appear every month for the next five months and that on 13 October she would perform a miracle which would be a sign that she had in fact appeared. On 13 October 1917 the sun danced in the sky, rain fell on the estimated 60,000 witnesses, yet no one was wet and the ground around where they stood was dry. We have been told we would have visions, they are happening and the word is being fulfilled, line upon line and precept upon precept. Some critics argue that the visionaries were just children. That is true. After Jesus cleared the temple of the money-changers and thieves He answered His critics, the chief priests and Scribes, "Have you never read. 'Out of the mouth of infants and sucklings Thou hast perfected praise?'"[161]

Most of the following information is from Father Gobbi's work, and where necessary I have included that date and the paragraph letter of the messages he has received from the Blessed Mother.

In opening for us the sealed books of the Apocalypse our Heavenly

Messenger enlightens us on the three beasts:

1. The great Red Dragon which is atheistic communism.[162]
2. The beast like a leopard which is Freemasonry.[163]
3. The beast like a lamb is Ecclesiastical Masonry infiltrated into the inner sanctum of the Roman Catholic Church.[164] It seeks to set up a false christ and a false church.

The three beasts are systems. The three beasts come under the control of a man, the Antichrist. The Antichrist will be preceded by the false prophet who hails the "liberation" produced by the three beasts rolled into one.

Russia and China are the centers of atheistic communism and its ominous dominance. Today many people are proclaiming "Peace, peace, but there is no peace."[165] Why is there so much concern about communism? The answer is that communism is the error foretold by Our Lady in 1917 before the Russian revolution. (See Appendix 2).

"And behold a great red dragon having seven heads and ten horns, and upon his heads seven diadems (crowns)."[166]

The great Red dragon is Marxist atheism, which appears with ten horns, that is with its power and its means of communication, in order to lead humanity to disobey the ten commandments of God. The horn, in the biblical world, has always been an instrument of amplification, a way of making one's voice better heard, a strong means of communication. Today it is the government controlled media.

The seven heads, upon each of which there is a crown, are signs of authority and royalty. The crowned heads indicate the nations in which atheistic communism is established and rules with the force of its ideological, political and military power.

Its color is red because it uses wars, torture, cruelty and blood as instruments of its numerous conquests. During this century it has succeeded in conquering humanity with the error of theoretical and practical atheism, which has now seduced all the nations of the earth. The Russians have courted the friendship of Libya, Iraq and Syria and have directly and indirectly financed the terrorist movements in the Middle East and elsewhere around the world. They are the prime supporters of the Palestinian Liberation Organization and in 1982 they were caught red handed when the Israelis discovered and captured arsenals of modern Russian weapons stashed in the caves and mountains of Lebanon, ready for a planned invasion of Israel. This was an ignominious defeat for the Russians (communism) and one which they want to revenge. They will be turned around with hooks in their jaws as we shall see in Chapter 8.

Communism as a system will collapse and those countries now under that type of rule will embrace the western style of "democracy." They will become subject to the Masonic dependence of voodoo economics and as such then, the great red dragon will give its own might and great authority to Freemasonry. The first beast of the Apocalypse Chapter 13 will hand over its system and authority to the beast like a leopard, the system of Masonic voodoo and deceit.

The beast like a leopard is Freemasonry. "The Dragon manifests himself in the force of his power; the leopard on the other hand acts in his shadow, keeps out of sight and hides himself in such a way as to enter in everywhere. He has the claws of a bear and the mouth of a lion, because he works with cunning and with the means of social communication, propaganda."[163]

"And I saw a beast coming up out of the sea, having seven heads and ten horns, and upon its horns ten diadems, and upon its heads blasphemous names. And the beast I saw was like a leopard, and its feet were like feet of a bear, and its mouth like the mouth of a lion. And the dragon gave it his own might and great authority. And one of its heads was smitten, as it were, unto death but its deadly wound was healed...And all the earth followed the beast in wonder. And they worshipped the dragon because he gave authority to the beast, and they worshipped the beast, saying, 'Who is like the beast, and who will be able to fight it?"[167]

This beast has ten horns and, on the horns, ten crowns, which are signs of dominion and royalty. Masonry rules and governs throughout the world by means of the ten horns. Most of those in power have sold their souls for power.

If the Red Dragon works to bring all humanity to do without God, to the denial of God...the aim of Masonry is not to deny God, but to blaspheme Him. As the beast like a leopard in the shadows it lurks and is always on the prowl, devouring. At once those in power have committed one indiscretion, they are at the mercy of their benefactor - Satan, Masonry.

God communicated His will to His people by means of ten horns which made His law known: the ten commandments. Because the Lord has communicated His law with the ten commandments, Freemasonry spreads everywhere, through the power of its ten horns, a law which is completely opposed to that of God.

To God's Commandments	Freemasonry opposes with:
1. Thou shalt not have any other God but Me.	False idols, before which many today prostrate themselves.
2. Thou shalt not take the name of God in vain.	Blasphemes God and His Christ, even to reducing His Name to the level of a brand-name of an object for sale and of producing sacrilegious films concerning His life and His Divine Person.
3. Remember to keep holy the Sabbath Days.	Sundays is a day of work, sports, competitions and entertainments.
4. Honor your father and your mother.	It opposes with a new model of family based on cohabitation, even between homosexuals.
5. You shall not commit impure acts.	It justifies, exalts and propagates every form of impurity, even to the justification of acts against nature.
6. You shall not kill.	It has approved contraception, made abortion legal, made euthanasia acceptable, and caused respect due to the value of human life all but disappear.
7. You shall not steal.	It works to the end that theft, violence, kidnapping and robbery spread more and more.
8. You shall not bear false witness.	The law of deceit, lying and duplicity becomes more and more propagated.
9 & 10. You shall not covet the goods and wife of another.	It works to corrupt the depths of conscience, betraying man's mind and heart.

God's grace of the redemption is communicated by means of the seven sacraments. With grace there becomes implanted in the soul the seeds of supernatural life which are seven virtues: faith, hope, charity, prudence, fortitude, justice and temperance.

The seven heads of the leopard indicate the various Masonic lodges, which act everywhere in a subtle and dangerous way to spread the opposite of the seven virtues, which are, the seven capital vices of, reason, flesh, money, discord, domination, violence and pleasure. On the head of every beast is written a blasphemous name. Each Masonic lodge has the task of making a different 'divinity' (vice) adored, to bring humanity everywhere to disdain the law of God, to work in open opposition to the ten commandments, and to take away the worship due to God alone in order to offer it to certain false idols which become extolled and adored by an ever increasing number of people. This becomes more evident as the TV ads become more obscene, as the news concentrates on corruption and the most grotesque scenes are shown without concern for the innocent mind.

To the Seven Virtues	Freemasonry counters with the Seven capital vices.
1. Faith.	Pride. Worship the god of human reason and haughtiness, of technology and progress.
2. Hope.	Lust. Offers worship to the god of sexuality and impurity.
3. Charity.	Greed. Worships the god of money.
4. Prudence.	Anger. Worships the god of discord and division.
5. Fortitude.	Sloth. Disseminates the worship of fear of public opinion and of exploitation.
6. Justice.	Envy. Offers worship to the idol of war and of violence.
7. Temperance.	Gluttony. Offers worship to the so highly extolled idols of hedonism, of materialism and of pleasure.

On 27 May 1917, just 14 days after Our Lady's first apparition at Fatima, the Roman Catholic Church officially condemned the Masonic sect under Canon 2335 which reads: "Persons joining associations of the Masonic sect or any others of the same kind which plot against the Church and legitimate civil authorities contract 'ipso facto' excommunication simply

51

reserved to the Apostolic See." In 1983 the Canon was updated to Canon 1374 which states "A person who joins an association which plots against the Church is to be punished with a just penalty; one who promotes or takes office in such an association is to be punished with an interdict."

The Masons see themselves as the masters of the universe. Looking back in history they delude themselves by thinking that they are the wisdom of the human race, characterized by the Satanic Eye of Providence. Using the symbols of the builders compass and square, they blasphemously claim to be the builders of the Egyptian Pyramids and King Solomon's Temple in Jerusalem. As they look to the future in their arrogance they see themselves as the predestined "Novus Ordo Seclorum," the "New World Order" and pretend to look toward an era of universal brotherhood and enlightenment...under their own definition.

Freemasonry is a revolutionary world-wide Satanic movement organized among other things:

1) To advance Kabbalistic Gnosticism. Briefly defined this is occult, with pretensions to esoteric religious insights emphasizing knowledge rather than faith and with a conviction that matter is evil. The New Age Movement is their prime spokes-organization.

2) To undermine and, if possible, to destroy Christianity, and in particular the Roman Catholic Church. It aims through its silent partner "The New Age Movement," to break the Christian Church into hundreds of various confessions emphasizing "reason" as opposed to "faith." Since the turn of this century alone, the number of "new" Christian churches have been staggering. Dissent and protest have been the voices of arrogance and pride, manifested for Masons by the occult of the New Age Movement on unsuspecting people. They insist that "Loyalty" to one's church and country has to be negated. They plan the destruction of all social influence by the Church and religions generally, either by open persecution or by so-called separation of Church and State. Through their New Age medium they blaspheme and ridicule God and His Christ and continue to attack the moral standards. Their aim is a false church and a false christ, their blasphemous totalitarian system. We shall deal with this later under the Beast like a Lamb.

3) To infuse Masonic philosophy into key government organizations and take control of all the governments of the world by subversion and whatever means necessary. By controlling religion, education, law and finance it could achieve its aims. Freemasonry is out to destroy God's gift

to man "...have dominion over the fishes of the sea, and the fowls of the air, and the beasts, and the whole earth, and every creeping creature that moveth upon the earth."[168] Because Satan is a beast and a creeping thing he must use whatever means he can to have victory over man. Lucifer would not serve man, and man will judge angels,[169] so Satan, a fallen angel, now has double iniquity, he is to be judged by man and he is to be overcome by man. "Bring upon them the day of affliction, and with a double destruction, destroy them."[170] Of Babylon (Satan) it is said, "Render to her as she also has rendered, and give her the double according to her works; in the cup that she has mixed, mix for her double."[135] By controlling man through greed and corruption, Satan is trying to condemn as many souls as possible to hell as his defiance in defeat.

4) To secularize all public and private life and, above all, public education. To systematically develop freedom of thought and conscience in school children, and protect them, so far as possible, against 'all disturbing influences of the Church, and even their own parents - by compulsion if necessary.' One of the greatest tools for violence, pornography and insatiable desires is the media and particularly television. Television is the idol spoken of in the Apocalypse 13:14, built to be adored by all nations on the earth, and to which Satan gives shape and movement so that it becomes in his hands, a terrible means of seduction and perversion for the children.

Under Presidents FDR, Truman and Eisenhower the appointment of Freemasons to the Supreme Court gave the antichrists the majority vote. As we referred to earlier, 1948 was an ominous year for the USA. The Supreme Court ruled in the Mc Collum case to ban any teaching of religion in public schools. This was just the beginning of the avalanche of laws against the children, and against God. In 1962 in the case of Engel Versus Vitale, prayer was removed from the public school. In that case there were no precedents, no previous legal cases or historical incidents cited in defense of their Anti-Christ decision. The prayer which was rendered 'unconstitutional' was, "Almighty God, we acknowledge our dependence upon Thee and we beg Thy blessings upon us, our parents, our teachers and our country." God is only mentioned once, the US Constitution mentions Him 4 times. In 1963 in the case of Abington V Schempp bible reading was outlawed. The court ruled that "If portions of the New Testament were read without explanation, they could be and had been psychologically harmful to a child." Again there were no legal or historical precedents cited. The attack continued, in 1965 no one could pray aloud in the public school. In 1980 the Ten Commandments and all religious pictures or charts had to be removed from public schools because

53

they were a "passive display" and could cause a person 'to think about God.'

For the purpose of gravity and to show the meaning of the verse of scripture which says "Behold I will bring evils upon this people, the fruits of heir own thoughts, because they have not heard My words, and THEY HAVE CAST AWAY MY LAW,"[171] I want to recall the economic picture and insert it here, adding the crime picture in the USA for the same period.

1934 FDR prohibits private ownership of gold. (This point is very important because the precedent has been established to prohibit the ownership of money. Next could be the dollar script).

1945 Gold reserves for Federal Reserve Notes and Deposits decreased from 35% to 25%

1948 Ban on teaching religion in public schools.

1962 Last year in which the 90% circulating silver coins were minted by the Government.

1962 Prayer in public schools prohibited.

1963 Bible reading prohibited in public schools.

1965 Praying "out loud" prohibited in public schools.

1968 Last 25% of gold reserves for Federal Reserve Notes and Deposits removed.

1971 Nixon ends international redeemability of Federal Reserve Note.

1980 All religious pictures and charts removed from schools.

1992 Budget had increased 760% in the past 20 years.

1992 US Bureau of Debt reported a 565% increase in the same 20 years.

1992 Per person share of National Debt increased 460%

1992 Minimum Wage increased just 165% compared to the governors increase of 760%

Since 1962 divorce rates have increased 120%. That is 50% of all marriages end in divorce.

Since 1962 the number of unmarried couples living together has increased 350%

Since 1962 teenage pregnancies has increased 550%

Since 1962 violent crime has increased 550%

Are we better off today than 20 years ago? Absolutely not. It really is true, the people must pay for the crimes of its country.

The establishment of Protestantism and Freemasonry is intertwined in an interesting way. Martin Luther (1483-1586) issued his thesis in 1517 and broke away from the Roman Catholic Church. King Henry VIII (1491-1547) wrote his "Defense of the Seven Sacraments" in answer to Luther

54

and received from Pope Leo X the title, "Fidei Defensor" (Defender of the Faith). This Papal title is still retained by the English monarchy to this very day and is inscribed on the British coins. Henry wanted to have the marriage to his wife, Catherine of Aragonne annulled. The request was denied. Henry rebelled, joined the Protestants, formed his own church, which he called the Church of England in 1523. He became the supreme head of the English Protestant Church, no longer was it the Church **IN** England, it became the Church **OF** England. He was now the head of the State and that church. Instead of the Church being the head of the State, the State was the head of the Church. For Henry, God had to render to Caesar.

Because of the break with the Church, the English masons, builders of the great stone buildings, especially the cathedrals, had lost their source of work. Over the next two hundred years the decline was excessive and so in 1717, in order to replenish the membership in their lodges, they recruited new members, particularly the "intellectuals" from the leading church, political, legal, educational, literary, commercial and monetary professions. The original members were all English Protestants. This is understandable since they were anti-Catholic and looked to the government (anti-Catholic) for favors.

In 1611 under the monarchy and patronage of King James the Protestants translated their own bible. Being a State church, they called their bible (with only 66 books) "The Authorised King James Version."

There is some misinformation about the Bible. The 27 Books of The New Testament were written by eight men under the inspiration of the Holy Spirit. If we are to take a chronological look at the important dates, allowing for understandable approximation for the first 100 years, we will see that the Apostles converted about 3,000 to the faith in one day,[172] and "the word of the Lord continued to spread, and the number of disciples increased rapidly in Jerusalem; a large number also of the priests accepted the faith,"[173] all without the Bible! They relied on oral tradition and as Saint John says in his Gospel, "There are, however, many other things that Jesus did; but if every one of these should be written, not even the world itself, I think, could hold the books that would have to be written. Amen."[174]

Let us look at when and where we got the Bible.

30 A.D.   (or 33 A.D.) Jesus crucified.
50   Earliest oral traditions of the Gospel put in written form.

	The first writings were not compiled until some 17 years after the death of Jesus.
	1 & 2 Thessalonians letters written.
56-58	Letter to Philippians, (this may have been written 61-63), 1 & 2 Corinthians, Galatians, & Romans.
61-63	Letters to Colossians, Ephesians, Philemon and 1 Timothy, Titus
	Gospel of Mark, 1 & 2 Peter,
	Letter of James
67	2 Timothy, Hebrews
70-80	Gospels of Matthew and Luke, Acts, and Letter of Jude.
95-98	Apocalypse (also called Revelation). Gospel of John, 1 John , (2 & 3 John may have been written earlier).
382	St. Jerome translated the New Testament consisting of the above 27 books into Latin at the request of Pope Saint Damascus (366-384). This translation became known as the 'Vulgate' which means the common or current accepted version.
397	Council of Carthage decreed the 27 books of the New Testament to be canon. This was approved and confirmed by Pope Saint Siricius (384-399).
404	Between 392 and 404 approximately, St. Jerome translated the Old Testament from Hebrew into Latin, except for the Psalms which he had revised earlier, a total of 46 books.
419	Second Council of Carthage, over which St. Augustine (354-430) presided, renewed the decrees of the First Carthage Council and declared that its act was to be notified to Pope Saint Boniface (418-422) for the purpose of confirmation. The entire Vulgate of 73 books was approved.

THE CHURCH GAVE US THE BIBLE
THE BIBLE DID NOT GIVE US THE CHURCH.

1442	Council of Florence. Reaffirmed 73 books of the Bible as canon (under Pope Eugene IV, 1431-1447).
1450	John Gooseflesh invents the Gutenberg printing press.
1452	The first printed book, the Bible, produced with about 200 copies of the Vulgate.
by 1500	Vulgate printed into the following editions; 14 German, 11 Italian, 10 French, 2 Bohemian, 1 Flemish, and 1 Russian.
by 1520	120 editions of the full 73 books of the Bible translated into Latin, plus 27 German, 40 Italian; in short there were "626 editions of the Bible, in which 198 were in the language of

the laity, with the insistence and the sanction of the Church in Rome, before the first Protestant version of the Scriptures was sent forth into the world."[175] The Catholic Bible has God in the beginning, "In the beginning, God..." has God at the end, "Come Lord Jesus...", and has God in the center, "the Lord our God" which are the mid-words from the mid-chapter, Psalms 122:2 (123:2 Hebrew numbering).

1520	Luther's first bible produced.
1546	Council of Trent (Pope Paul III) upheld and restated earlier councils on the canon of 73 books of the Bible.
1582	Douay Rheims English Translation of the New Testament.
1609	Douay Rheims Translation of the Old Testament, full canon of 46 books.
1611	King James Authorised Protestant Version.

"The Authorised King James Version" was published some 29 years after the Catholic Douay Rheims English translation and some 159 years after the first printed Catholic Bible!

In accepting only 66 books in their bible, the Protestants took their Old Testament canon from the Pharisees who set up four criteria for establishing the Jewish canon.

1. They had to be in harmony with the Pentateuch, the first five books of the bible.
2. They had to be written before the time of Ezra. (Sirach and Macabees were written after that).
3. They had to be written in Hebrew. (Judith, parts of Daniel and Esther were written in Aramaic, Wisdom was written in Greek).
4. They had to be written in Israel. (Baruch was written in exile in Babylon).

The authority for the 39 books of the Hebrew canon is a matter of debate. Some attribute it to Ezra and Nehemiah at about 430 B.C., others to 100 B.C.; we do know however that at the Synod of Jabneh (Jamnia or Jabneel) at about 100 A.D. the Hebrews affirmed their 39 books.

Without further historical analysis there is one question that should be kept in mind. If the Jews did not accept Jesus as the Messiah, and "we for our part preach a crucified Christ - to the Jews indeed a stumbling block,"[176] why should Christians restrict their canon by those for whom Jesus is a 'stumbling block?' The significance of this error will become more evident when we examine the World Council of Churches as a "religious" forum for the Antichrist. We shall see later that Antichrist will want to deny that Jesus Christ the Messiah ever came on earth. He will proclaim himself the Messiah and the Jews will accept him. By starting off using their canon with only 39 books, it is easy to see how much more readily Antichrist will be accepted by the Jews and those who deny Christ.

Luther further distanced himself from the Roman Catholic Church, by considering "...his interpretation of St. Paul was the criterion for all New Testament books. On this basis he formed three groups; Romans, Galatians and John; the other NT books, including the Synoptics, he relegated to second place; he severely censured Hebrews, Jude, 2nd Peter and Apocalypse, while he called James 'a straw epistle.'"[177]

The Protestants are noted for their lack of acceptance of oral tradition, contrary to 2 Thessalonians 2:15, and a degrading of the importance of Mary, the Mother of Jesus, contrary to John 19:27. This fact becomes most important when three particular years are studied:

1517 Luther's Revolt,
1717 Freemasonry formalized, and
1917 Three major events took place:

FIRST. Mary, the Mother of Jesus, appeared six times at Fatima on 13th of each month from May through October except for August when the children were detained by the local police and she visited them on the 19th. It is worth noting here that Fatima was the name of the daughter of Mohammed the founder of Islam. In the Koran, which means "The Recital" and which Moslems believe to be the word of God, dictated to Mohammed by the Angel Gabriel, the Blessed Mother is mentioned in suras, which means chapters, 3, 19, 21, 23 & 66 a total of 34 times. 23 of those times her name is linked with her Son, Jesus. No other name except Moses, Abraham and Noah appears so often, and Mary's is the only mention of a personal name of a WOMAN in the entire Koran. It is this writer's personal belief that it will be through Mary that the Islamic nations will be brought to Jesus, and it is no small 'coincidence' that Our Blessed Mother Mary appeared at "Fatima." Mohammed had no sons (Sura 33:40) and Fatima was the family heiress. Mohammed's inheritance went to Fatima! Mary conquered Fatima and so all Islam must bow down to her.

SECOND. The end of the Islamic dominance in Israel (Palestine) with the Balfour Declaration on 2nd November 1917 (just 19 days after the last apparition at Fatima), and the freedom of Jerusalem as we have seen in

Chapter 3.

THIRD. At Fatima Our Blessed Mother prophesied "Russia's Error" months before the Russian Revolution which started on 6 November '17. Russia's error was and is atheistic communism, promulgated by Freemasonry, born of "secular humanism," whose father is Satan, and was first inflicted upon the human race by the devil in the Garden of Eden when he said "You shall be as Gods."

The agitation which began in the 1300's with the advent of Albigensianism, which essentially denied the presence of the Holy Spirit in a body, and held that Christ or God could not have had a real human body and consequently there could be no resurrection of the body, grew into the revolt by Luther, into the establishment of the State church by King Henry VIII, and finally into the Communist Godless and Churchless State which came about in Russia and China. This however, is not yet the ultimate plan of the Antichrist; his goal is a godless and churchless world, with Satan as god.

Let us see how this has developed and where it is at today.

CHAPTER 8

THE NEW WORLD ORDER

Today we hear a lot about "The New World Order." After the apparent victory of United Nations forces, or The Alliance of Nations as they were legally called, the term "New World Order" has come to be accepted as readily as "USA." The New World Order is not something born in 1991. No, it was born by deceit in the garden of Eden, as we have seen earlier.

In order to have a "New World Order" there was first needed "The New World." When the "Pilgrims" came to America in 1620 they had among their members those truly devoted to freedom. Within one hundred years, that is immediately after the formalizing of Freemasonry in London in 1717, immigrants from England would arrive in America carrying the Freemasonry ideals . "The New World," according to Freemasons was founded for "The New World Order." Patience and planning would bring about the sinister satanic designs in due course. In the intervening 270 years the goals of a godless society would be almost completed by:

a) forbidding the one true God of revelation to be worshipped in schools and public places,
b) enslavement of a people in a taxation system which would leave them always at the mercy of the government,
c) the destruction of Biblical morals in favor of human judgment, and
d) a legal system in place of a justice system.

In order to make the "New World Order" an absolute authority, there would be needed three major forums in which to operate and control the political, monetary and religious systems. In the political system it is necessary for Communism to collapse as a world force. In the monetary system it is necessary for all the nations to be indebted to one entity. In the religious system it is necessary for a mass movement toward "liberalism" and also the destruction of the Catholic Church. Basically the ingredients for these three parts of this super system can now be found in the United Nations, the World Bank, and the World Council of Churches, the umbrella for The New Age Movement.

THE UNITED NATIONS is the ideal and established forum of Freemasonry. Headquartered in New York, or the New Quarter, the setting was the main entry point of "The New World." There, the politics of the few are impressed upon all. This body has its own morality and code, and has in the various countries of the world such clandestine entities as The Council of Foreign Relations. The Seven Industrial Nations, known today as the Group of Seven or G-7, are the controlling governments behind the United Nations. I speculate that these seven nations are the "seven thunders" of Revelation,[178] that they are also the "seven heads" and that the Soviet Union (Russia) "is at the same time the eighth and one of the seven..."[179]

When the United Nations went to war against Iraq in January 1991, it did so under UN Resolution Numbers ranging from 660, 661, 662, 664, 665, 666 (on the 13th day of the 9th month 1990), 667, 669, 670, 674, and 678! These UN resolution numbers are assigned in sequential numbers as they come up. (For Resolution 666 giving the United Nations Security Council control over foodstuffs see appendix 3).

China was persuaded, through "the invisible government by the money power," the economic rulers of the world, not to side with Iraq and so it abstained from voting. Later it would get a most favored nation trading status from the USA in return for its co-operation! Russia voted for the resolution, and agreed with the warring alliance, but did not join forces with it. How could it fight against itself? They kept their advisors in Iraq to fight against the technology of the "Alliance." Some ally! After the 'war,' Russia moved diplomatically and won third-world respect for its 'peace initiatives' and 'humane' ending of hostilities. A deal was cut between the 'rulers of the world.'

The US, the EEC, Russia and China are able to put their great might and authority together to dictate to all the inhabitants of this earth what they must do. They control the UN and operate under the influence of the beast like a leopard, Freemasonry. "Who is like the beast, and who will be able to fight it?"[180] We know the geography of Iraq and that the river Euphrates flows through it, except for that part in the east which borders Iran. When the bombs started falling we were alerted that the angel had started pouring the sixth bowl of wrath. "The sixth angel poured out his bowl upon the river Euphrates, and dried up its waters, that a way might be made ready for the kings from the rising sun. And I saw issuing from the mouth of the dragon, and from the mouth of the beast, three unclean spirits like frogs (Evil governments, voodoo economics and a godless religion). For they are the spirits of demons working signs, and they go forth unto the kings of the whole earth to gather them together for the battle on the great day of God Almighty. And He gathered them together in a place that is called in Hebrew Armageddon."[181] The three unclean spirits are the dragon, the beast and the false church and these three are under the command of the UN. Armageddon is in northern Israel, and the UN resolutions 660 - 678 are still active. The action against Iraq is not concluded. "Kings from the rising sun" signifies nations from all over the world, the UN. It should be noted that through economic persuasions, Israel stayed out of the war even though her borders were violated. Israel agreed to the "Alliance" demand that US troops be stationed in Israel to "protect" her. The "Alliance" used persuasively its great power so that no one could resist. Through economics, "the invisible government by the money power" made its statement, made its demand and Israel acceded in return for promised paper dollars! "Who is like the beast, and who will be able to fight it?"

The prophet Ezekiel says, "Behold I come against thee O Gog...And I will turn thee about, and I will put a bit in thy jaws, and I will bring thee forth, and all thy army...a great multitude...the Persians, the Ethiopians, and Libyans with them...Gomer and all his bands, the house of Thogorma, the northern parts and all his strength, and many peoples with thee."[182] Gog signifies hidden, secret or covered and refers to Antichrist. Freemasonry is hidden and secret as we have seen, and it controls the UN. It will hand over authority to one person, the Antichrist, into whose jaws the Lord will put a bit or "hooks" (NJB). Magog is the armies and nations attached to him, so under the UN all is in place. "In the day of the coming of Gog upon the land of Israel, declares The Lord God, that My indignation shall come up in My wrath...I will call in the sword against him...every man's sword shall be pointed against his brother. And I will judge him with pestilence, and with blood, and with violent rain, and vast hailstones: I will rain fire and brimstone upon him, and upon his army, and upon the many nations that are with him."[183]

THAT PART OF THE PROPHECY, "GOMER AND ALL HIS BANDS," INCLUDES THE UNITED NATIONS. It is interesting to note that fire and brimstone have already fallen on the USA's Philippine air base in June '91, and the greatest army in the world withdrew without being able to fire a shot. "Not with an army, nor by might, but by My Spirit, says the Lord of Hosts."

The UN armed forces have been used in many places throughout the world in what is termed "police actions." We have come to accept this terminology which is a very subtle danger. The countries controlling the UN and in particular the US, Russia, UK and France have sent their secret service, the CIA, KGB etc. into those countries which they individually dominate and have trained the local police force and intelligence units in the most hideous forms of cruelty and repression. These tactics will be used in the days ahead in a most sinister fashion. The ugly scenes flashed on TV showing an Israeli army unit pistol whipping a Palestinian; or the Los Angeles police publicly brutalizing a "black suspect;" or the British Army indiscriminately murdering Irish citizens; or South African police mass killing black township residents; or the Russian Army killing provincials in Lithuania and Moldova are merciful in comparison to what goes on behind the prison doors and torture chambers. These armies and police forces will come under the UN police control in the New World Order.

Thankfully, the New World Order will be short lived and it is going to its destruction and it's demise is already foretold, "On that Day, declares the Lord, uproar will be heard from the Fish Gate (at the entrance across the Thames river to the City of London), wailing from the New Quarter, (New York) and a great crash from the hills. Wail you who live in the Hollow (Wall Street), for it is all over with the merchants (stock markets), all the money-bags have been wiped out."[184]

THE WORLD BANK. In order to have a world monetary system, it is necessary to have a commonly accepted currency. The USA dollar is presently such a currency. The voodoo money system of Freemasonry is in place under the eye of the World Bank which approves or disapproves of the economic activities of all the nations and most of the sovereign states! The world is now becoming cashless, that is without money. Because the governments of the world are bankrupt, to whom do they owe the money? "The borrower is the lender's slave,"[150] so who is the lender? Is he "invisible?" "For it is not against human enemies that we have to struggle, but against the principalities and the ruling forces who are masters of the darkness in this world, the spirits of evil in the heavens"[185] A former chairman of the Federal Reserve Board is now the "advisor" to the Russian Government.

THE WORLD COUNCIL OF CHURCHES was formed in Amsterdam in 1948. This was Satan's answer to Israel regaining sovereignty in 1948 as we saw in Chapter 3. God gave us the One True Church founded on Jesus Christ. The World Council of Churches seeks to deceive people by proclaiming that each "DEnomination" has something of value to offer. They choose what they consider to be of value and veil everything on "ecumenism." They use the word "DEnomination," yet we know that since God "nominates," Satan "DE-nominates." This "World" Council forgets "Who is there that overcomes the WORLD if not he who believes that Jesus is the Son of God?"[186] Today this World Council of Churches has a committee which is making an "intellectual" critique of the Bible with a

63

view of "correcting" and updating it for "our time." The precedent was set at the Reformation and continues today. The reformers denied the canon which had been established since the beginning of the published bible (382 A.D.). Their canon has five books of wisdom contrary to proverbs, "Wisdom hath built herself a house, she hath hewn her out seven pillars."[187] As recently as early 1991, a committee decided that most of what was written in the Bible as quotes from Jesus could not have been so, and it refuted the Biblical authenticity. The king, Freemasonry, "growing more and more arrogant...considers himself greater than all the gods...utters incredible blasphemies against the God of gods will thrive until the wrath reaches bursting point."[188] This false church is promoting "faith" by "reason only." If it is 'reason only,' then it is not 'faith.' The Church Council of the "World" is the ideal smokescreen for Freemasonry's attack using the New Age Movement. This false church is soon to have its ranks swelled from the apostasy, the 'great revolt' by those Catholics who cannot accept the authority of the True Church. With the canon distorted, Jesus denied, the way is prepared for the arrival of the Antichrist and his lying wonders which "make fire come down from heaven upon mankind in the sight of mankind,"[189] but they are not "wonders" in the sight of God they are phoney.

Until recently Masons had a monthly magazine called "THE NEW AGE" for their members. This propaganda piece is one of the American "horns" of the beast like a leopard. It extols those who follow Masonry and gives them "crowns" or "diadems." It is the satanic voice for the New Age Movement. The "New Age Movement" is not something born in this generation, no, its very origins go back to the birth of secular humanism in the Garden of Eden. Satan, its founder, convinced Eve that if she ate of the tree of knowledge she would be as "God." "Now the serpent was more subtle than any of the beasts of the earth which the Lord God made...And the serpent said to the woman: 'No, you shall not die the death. For God doth know that in what day soever you shall eat thereof your eyes shall be opened and you shall be as Gods, knowing good and evil."[190] When she and Adam ate that fruit, in that moment "Secular Humanism" was born, and from that time "The New Age Movement" has been trying to establish itself over all the world and in this year, 1992, Secular Humanism and The New Age Movement are cooperating together to form a subtle, sinister "NEW WORLD ORDER." Under this guise, Satan is trying to set up his world of darkness to try to discredit, disgrace and disavow the New and Eternal Covenant of Our Lord and Savior Jesus Christ.

The New Age Movement is a gathering together of pseudo "intellectuals" who are attempting to rewrite the order of the ages as set up by God The

Creator. They no longer see man and woman as distinctive people, but only as 'persons.' They carry their silly analysis of terminology such as waiter or waitress to "waitperson," and chairman or chairwoman to "chairperson." In submission to the feminists and homosexuals, they support unnatural associations and rebel at established authority, "Their courage exhausted, they are now like women."[191] They further rebel at those men and women, who question or challenge their newly established and enforced authority. They are an authority unto themselves and are willing and ready to kill, murder, plunder and rob in order to enforce their warped ideals. Operating under the demonic spell of Satan, these poor unfortunates see only darkness from their evil tower. Witchcraft, devil worship, seances and black masses form their cult; murder of innocents is their highest form of occult. They have seduced the minds of many potentially good people who want to be 'accepted' and so wrongfully follow their evil seduction. Shortly, this vile force is to join totally with Communism and Freemasonry under the leadership of "the Lawless One," the man of perdition.

These two systems will give authority to that one person, Gog, the Antichrist, who will rule the world. Just as God The Father gave all power and authority to His Son, Jesus Christ, so too will Satan give all power and authority on earth to his elected son of sin, the Antichrist.[192] Just as The Father and Son have sent The Holy Spirit to inspire the faithful, so too the devil has sent the evil spirit to persuade the people to follow the Antichrist and the system is now in place. Satan seeks complete authority over all the nations, and he has almost succeeded in achieving this. "Arrogance and outrage are now ascendant; it is a period of turmoil and bitter hatred."[193] As we have seen earlier, the satanic trinity was released when the bombs dropped on the Euphrates.

Satan almost has control over the whole world, but not completely over every country because the True Church still exists and "the gates of hell shall not prevail against it."[194] At the height of its arrogance, Freemasonry must be overcome by the meek "who shall inherit the earth." The prophesy will then be fulfilled because the seventh angel said **"THE KINGDOM OF THE WORLD HAS BECOME THE KINGDOM OF OUR LORD AND HIS CHRIST,** and He will reign for ever and ever,"[195] and Jesus "will give the authority over the nations" to His elect, which authority He has been given by our Father, "...to rule them with an iron septre and shatter them like so many pots."[196]

We talk a lot about "THE MEEK' and most people think of meek as meaning wimp or weakling. This is not so. Meek means one who is patient and mild, not inclined to anger or resentment, one who stands his ground knowing he is right.

Two miracles recorded by Saint Mark, Chapter 5, are very significant in political terms today. The two cures were to women. The two cures involve 12 years. The United States is referred to in the feminine as are most countries of the world. The United States is hemorrhaging from sin and all kinds of impurities. This is the first woman of the miracles. The significance of "12" in sacred numbers is "government." Our United States Government should lead the war against "liberal liberties" and lead the country in prayer and fasting on a national scale for five days.

The second female in the miracles is 12 years old and again this young girl represents all the slaughtered children by abortion, with the permission and funding of the Federal and State Governments. (Abortion is a very anti-septic word which is substituted for "kill").

"There came one of the rulers of the synagogue named Jarius. Seeing Jesus he fell at His feet...saying, 'My daughter is at the point of death, come, lay Thy hands upon her, that she may be saved and live.' And He went away with him.

And there was a woman who for 12 years had a hemorrhage, and had suffered much at the hands of many physicians...but rather grew worse. Hearing about Jesus she came up behind Him and touched His cloak. For she said, 'If I touch but His cloak, I shall be saved.' And at once the flow of her blood was dried up...And Jesus, instantly perceiving in Himself that power had gone forth from Him, turned to the crowd, and said, 'Who touched My cloak?'...The woman, fearing and trembling, knowing what had happened within her, came and fell down before Him, and told Him all the truth. But He said to her, 'Daughter, thy faith has saved thee. Go in peace, and be thou healed of thy affliction.'

While He was yet speaking, there came some from the house of the ruler of the synagogue, saying, 'Thy daughter is dead'...But Jesus...said to the ruler of the synagogue, 'Do not be afraid, only have faith'...And going in He said to them...The girl is asleep, not dead.' And they laughed Him to scorn...He entered in where the girl was lying. And taking the girl by the hand, He said to her, 'Girl, I say to thee, arise.' And the girl rose up immediately and began to walk, she was 12 years old. And they were utterly amazed...And He...directed that something be given her to eat."[197]

What a wonderful example it would be to all the citizens of the United States, to all the leaders of the world and to all the citizens of the world, if they could see the President of the great United States of America humble himself before God and lead the people of his country in prayer and fasting. That kind of example is expected and received from our religious leaders. That kind of example is not expected from our political leaders because we generally associate them with dishonesty, distortion and distress. The President could seize the opportunity to distinguish himself with honesty, truth and joy before God...active service, not lip service. Jesus can heal us of our sins, He can purify us, and He wants the country to turn to Him, our Merciful Savior. "And My people, upon whom My name is called, being converted, shall make supplication to Me, and seek out My face, and do penance for their most wicked ways, then I will hear from heaven, and will forgive their sins and will heal their land."[198]

When we are told to pray for our leaders we have to be serious about that prayer. Our leaders need prayer more than we or they think. I do not say this in a snide way, but in a sincere and heartfelt cry. We as a nation have a president and vice-president today who have been born and bred into a system not of their own making. They have inherited a bureaucracy from former mismanagement and which is entrenched in the attitude that 'this is the way we always did it.' Perpetrating a system they know is corrupt and being corrupted they are leading and being led astray 'for lack of knowledge.' As a Catholic I pray for our leaders and all those in positions of authority. It is easy to criticize and make fun of our politicians, but they are the inheritors of the actions of their political ancestors who have given us the present set of unacceptable standards. God advises these politicians, "The just considers seriously the house of the wicked, that he may withdraw the wicked from evil."[199]

"Wisdom is better than strength, and a wise man is better than a strong man. Hear therefore, ye kings, and understand; learn, ye that are judges of the ends of the earth. Give ear, you that rule the people, and that please yourselves in multitudes of nations; for power is given to you by the Lord, and strength by the Most High, Who will examine your works, and search out your thoughts, because being ministers of His kingdom, you have not judged rightly, nor kept the law of justice, nor walked according to the will of God. Horribly and speedily will He appear to you, for a most severe judgment shall be to them that bear rule. For to him that is little, mercy is granted, but the mighty shall be mightily tormented."[200] That is strong medicine and so, in love for all our brothers, we must pray for the leaders. "I urge therefore, first of all, that supplications, prayers, intercessions and thanksgivings be made for all men; for kings, and for all in high positions, that we may lead a quiet and peaceful life in all piety and worthy behavior. This is good and agreeable in the sight of God our Savior, Who wishes all men to be saved and to come to the knowledge of truth."[201] I call upon the President, Vice President and all the Cabinet and their families and invite them to join the Roman Catholic Church where the fullness of the promises of Jesus Christ awaits them. "Let everyone be subject to higher authorities, for there exists no authority except from God, and those who exist have been appointed by God."[202]

As a Catholic, I heed the commandments, "be subject to princes and authorities, obeying commands, ready for every good work, speaking evil of none, not quarrelsome but moderate, showing all mildness to all men. For we ourselves also were once unwise, unbelieving, going astray, slaves to various lusts and pleasures, living in malice and envy, hateful and hating one another."[203] "Be subject to every human creature for God's sake, whether to the king as supreme, or to governors as sent through him for vengeance on evildoers and for the praise of the good. For such is the will of God, that by doing good you should put to silence the ignorance of foolish men. Honor all men; love the brotherhood; fear God; honor the king."[204] It is right to pray for leaders and all people. It is right and just to pray for their conversion from a futile way of life. Unity, love and kindness are the marks of God's people who will have come out of Babylon and escaped to places of refuge which God has prepared for His faithful,[205] and where there will be shade from the heat by day and refuge and shelter from the storm and rain. The Lord is "faithful to the faithful, blameless to the blameless, sincere to the sincere but cunning to the crafty, you save a people that is humble and humiliate those with haughty looks."[206] Has the current President the courage to declare that the present economic system is voodoo? He called it by the same name when he was challenging Mr. Reagan for the Republican presidential nomination in 1980. He is the prime supporter of that same voodoo today. Truthful? Inconsistent? In bondage? Was it a thirst for power which made him oppose it in 1980, or a thirst for power that makes him propose it in 1992? Or, does this CIA trained executive, expert in covert operations not know better. Does he have the courage to throw off the shackles of repression?

Why would the enemy, Freemasonry, Communism, Voodoo economics and the World Council of Churches fight among themselves? "And the ten horns that thou sawest, and the beast, these will hate the harlot, and will make her desolate and naked, and will eat her flesh, and burn her up in fire. For God has put it into their hearts to carry out His purpose, to give their kingdom to the beast, until the words of God are accomplished. And the woman thou sawest is the great city which has kinship over the kings of the earth."[207] Let us examine antichrists and the Antichrist.

CHAPTER 9

THE ANTICHRIST

There are many antichrists, but there is one who will be known as the Antichrist. He is the viper, the serpent, the beast, the Lawless one, the cruel one, the wicked one, he is the 666.

We hear some people saying that the Antichrist is this person or that person. We have heard all sorts of names of modern people and such speculation is rubbish and those individuals offering such false information are deceitful and are themselves antichrists. That the Antichrist is a man cannot be disputed,[208] and he will be revealed when The Lord wills it.[209]

Who or what is the Antichrist?

"I saw another beast coming up out of the earth, and it had two horns like those of a lamb, but it spoke as does a dragon. It exercised all the authority of the former beast in its sight; and it made the earth and the inhabitants therein to worship the first beast, whose deadly wound was healed."[210]

The lamb in holy scripture has always been a symbol of sacrifice. On the night of the exodus, the lamb is sacrificed and the doorposts of the houses of the Hebrews are sprinkled with its blood, in order to remove them from the punishment which would strike all the Egyptians. The Hebrew Pasch recalls this fact each year through the immolation of a lamb which is sacrificed and consumed. On Calvary, Jesus Christ sacrifices Himself for the redemption of humanity; He Himself becomes our Pasch and becomes the true Lamb of God who takes away all the sins of the world.

The beast like a lamb has on its head "two horns like those of a lamb." To the symbol of the sacrifice there is intimately connected that of the priesthood, the two horns. The high priest of the Old Testament wore a headpiece with two horns.[211] The bishops of the Church wear the mitre - with two horns - to indicate the fullness of their priesthood.

The beast like a leopard indicates Freemasonry; the beast with two horns like a lamb indicates Freemasonry infiltrated into the interior of the Church which is termed "Ecclesiastical Masonry," and has spread among some members of the hierarchy. The task of Masonry is to lead souls to perdition, bringing them to worship false divinities. The task of ecclesiastical Masonry on the other hand is that of destroying Christ and His Church, building a new idol, namely, a false christ and a false church, like the World Council of Churches.

Ecclesiastical Masonry works to obscure the Divine Word of Jesus by means of natural and rational interpretations and, in the attempt to make it more understandable and acceptable, empties it of faith and all its supernatural content. This loss of faith is apostasy and is the 'revolt' spoken of in Thessalonians.[71] Ecclesiastical Masonry works, in a subtle and diabolical way, to lead all into apostasy. Its aim is that of justifying sin, of presenting it no longer as an evil but as something good and of value. "In those days...everyone did that which seemed right to himself."[212] They will convince many that fair is foul and foul is fair, but Jesus says "I am going to make the synagogue of Satan, those who falsely claim to be Jews, but are liars, because they are no such thing - I will make them fall at your feet and recognize that I have loved you."[213]

After having tried to destroy the historical Christ, the beast with two horns like a lamb seeks to destroy the mystical Christ which is the Church. It seeks to destroy this reality through false ecumenism, which leads to the acceptance of all Christian churches, asserting that each one of them has some part of truth. It develops the plan of founding a universal ecumenical church, formed by the fusion of all Christian confessions, including the Catholic Church into something like the World Council of Churches. We have seen earlier their distortions of the Bible, both in rejecting the Catholic canon and denying the word of Jesus.

The Roman Catholic Church is life because it gives grace and it alone possesses the efficacious means of grace, which are the seven sacraments (Baptism, Confession, Eucharist, Confirmation, Matrimony, Holy Orders, Extreme Unction, now called Anointing of the sick). Especially it is life because to it alone is given the power to beget the Eucharist, by means of the hierarchical and ministerial priesthood. In the Eucharist, Jesus Christ is truly present with His glorified Body and His Divinity. We shall see in Chapter 11 the developing significance of the eucharist when the Eucharistic Reign of Christ reaches its fullness. And so ecclesiastical Masonry, in many subtle ways, seeks to attack the ecclesial devotion towards the sacrament of the Eucharist. It gives value only to the meal aspect, tends to minimize its sacrificial value and seeks to deny the real and personal presence of Jesus in the consecrated Host. Already in some American churches which call themselves "Catholic," the priest throws the consecrated Hosts into the garbage at the end of Mass denying the True Presence and preaching only the meal aspect of the service. "Son of man,

70

say to her, 'You are a land that has not received rain or shower on the day of anger. In you the princes are like a roaring lion tearing at its prey, They have eaten the people, seized wealth and jewels and widowed many inside her."[214]

By irreverence and attitudes of 'just a meal,' there are gradually suppressed all the external signs which are indicative of faith in the real presence of Jesus in the Eucharist, such as genuflections, hours of public adoration and the holy custom of surrounding the tabernacle with lights and flowers. The misguided people will deny the "real presence" in the Eucharist saying it is impossible for bread to become the "real presence" of Jesus. They will avoid discussing the "real presence" in the Ark of the Covenant because the Antichrist will want to win the Jews to his cause.

The Roman Catholic Church is the way because it leads to the Father, through the Son, in the Holy Spirit, along the way of perfect unity. The Church succeeds in being united because it has been founded on the cornerstone of its unity: Peter, and the Pope who succeeds to the charism of Peter. Ecclesiastical Masonry seeks to destroy the foundation of the unity of the Church through a subtle and insidious attack on the Pope. "In those days, there was no king in Israel, but everyone did that which seemed right."[215] Ecclesiastical Masonry will seek to remove the Pope.

Ecclesiastical Masonry receives orders and power from the various Masonic lodges and works to lead everyone secretly to become part of these secret sects. Thus it stimulates the ambitious with the prospect of easy careers; it heaps up with goods those who are starved for money; it assists its members to exceed others and to occupy the most important positions while it sets aside, in a subtle but decisive way, all those who refuse to take part in its designs. Indeed the beast like a lamb exercises all its power from the first beast, in its presence, and it forces the earth and all its inhabitants to adore the first beast. Remember again that the three beasts are systems and the Antichrist forcing adoration of a false system, assisted by the false prophet. The greed for power will force this false prophet to be the mouthpiece for Satan. In 1738 Pope Clement XII described Freemasonry as "Satan's synagogue." The Apocalypse states "And to the angel of the church at Smyrna write: Thus says the First and the Last, who was dead and is alive: I know thy tribulation and thy poverty, but thou art rich and that thou art slandered by those who say they are Jews and are not, but are a synagogue of Satan."[216]

Following the identification of the Antichrist there will come terrible persecutions and martyrdom against the little flock, the faithful remnant.

71

Through the World Council of Churches, the Antichrist will attempt to abolish the Roman Catholic Church, make it illegal and punishable by death for anyone to belong to or practice the faith. Already the United Nations in November 1981 have declared their power over religion. (see Appendix 4). On 25 November, the General Assembly of the United Nations General Assembly adopted without vote the "Declaration on the Elimination of All Forms of Intolerance and of Discrimination Based on Religion or Belief." It is interesting to note that "Iran said the United Nations was a secular body, and secular bodies were not qualified to deal with religious matters; Iran accepted the Declaration in so far as it was in **TOTAL CONFORMITY WITH ISLAMIC JURISPRUDENCE.**"[217] This Iranian Moslem condemnation and endorsement alone should alert all Christendom to be aware of the deadly peril contained in this rather subtle and seemingly innocuous "Declaration." We shall see shortly the connection between Islam and the Antichrist.

"From the time when the continual sacrifice shall be taken away, and the abomination unto desolation shall be set up there shall be a thousand two hundred and ninety days."[218] The 'continual sacrifice' is the Catholic celebration of the Mass, the Holy Eucharist ("do this in remembrance of Me").[219] By gradually permitting secular people to be 'Eucharistic Ministers,' (which by Church law are to be allowed only in exceptional circumstances), and by allowing the reception of holy communion in the hand, there is a gradual but subtle move to lead souls away from the Eucharist and its full meaning. In time, most of them will not object to the complete removal of the Eucharist and the replacement with a cafeteria type meal.

"Therefore when you see the abomination of desolation, which was spoken of by Daniel the prophet, standing in the holy place - let him who reads understand..."[217] and be aware! Under the New World Order's UN police force, the cruelty unleashed upon the citizenry will be beastly. Electronic torture, chemical injected brutality will make the events of Nero, Henry VIII, Cromwell, Stalin and Hitler look timid. "For then there will be great tribulation, such as has not been from the beginning of the world until now, nor will be. And unless those days had been shortened, no living creature would be saved. But for the sake of the elect those days will be shortened."[220] The man of iniquity will lay siege to the Vatican and move with all the power of 666 to Jerusalem to rule with terror and hatred. This one individual will incorporate in his person the totality of all cruelty, hatred, vile and deceitfulness. He is totally possessed by Satan and is Satan's imperfect attempt at becoming incarnate.

To better understand how Atheistic Communism and Freemasonry take control of an individual, let us first understand how the number 666 come about and from where it derived its origins?

It has been stated that the numbers are the Greek word for Roman, LATEINOS. In the Greek lettering L=30, A=1, T=300,E=5,I=10, N=50, O=70, S=200, sum = 666. Other interesting combinations include the man made computer, which when taken in the English language and assigning the number 6 for the letter A, and increasing each letter by 6, then the word COMPUTER = 666. The largest computer in the world is in the EEC Headquarters in Brussels, the re-birthed Roman Empire! To expound on the possible combinations equalling 666 would be an exercise in futility, but we should not close our eyes to 'things...ordered in number,'[80] as we have seen earlier.

In determining the overall significance of 666, in my estimation the key is to focus on 600, then 60 and finally the unit 6. Let us take a look! "Noah was 600 years old when the flood came...In the 600th year of Noah's life, in the second month, and on the seventeenth day of the month...Noah...boarded the ark."[221]

Our present creation began with Noah, "God saw that human wickedness was great on earth and that his heart contrived wickedness all day long...But Noah won the Lord's favor...Noah was a good man, an upright man among his contemporaries, and he walked with God...God said to Noah, 'I have decided that the end has come for all living things for the earth is full of lawlessness because of human beings...'"[222] "It was in the 601st year of Noah's life, in the first month and on the first of the month...Noah lifted back the hatch of the ark and looked out. The surface of the ground was dry."[223] All previous wickedness was destroyed and we begin our generation with Noah from his 601st year on the 1st day of the 1st month. Noah is the father of this present creation. Like Adam and his descendants, Noah's descendants sinned. We have sinned.

We will pay particular attention to the tribe of Dan. Dan was the first of two sons born to Jacob's concubine Bilhah. "Jacob called his sons and said, 'Gather round, so that I can tell you what is in store for you in the FINAL DAYS...May Dan be a snake on the road, a viper on the path, who bites the horse on the hock so that its rider falls off backwards!'"[224]

This was a rather strange tiding to Dan, calling him a snake and a viper. Why would a rider fall backwards? The hock is the heel of the horse, and if the rider falls off backwards then the horse must have reared up lifting its front legs in the air. If it reared up on its hind legs, then the danger must have been in front of it. If the danger was in front of it then the rider must have trusted it. If the rider trusted it then the adversary would have had secret and evil intentions from the onset. The snake attacked the unsuspecting person from the front pretending friendship. This is what we are to expect from Dan in the FINAL DAYS. Freemasonry, feigning friendship and fun loving philanthropy will attack the unsuspecting world from the front. Jesus was betrayed by a kiss from a "friend."

The Masonic New Age literature describes the serpent as "a symbol of wisdom...serpent worship in some form has permeated nearly all parts of the earth...the serpent is the symbol and prototype of the Universal Savior, who redeems the world...the Serpent Kings founded the Mystery Schools which later appeared as the Egyptian and Brahmin Mysteries...The serpent was their symbol...They were the true Sons of Light, and from them have descended a long line of adepts and initiates duly tried and proven according to the law."[225] Since Lucifer WAS "light," these are now the sons of Satan, now "darkness." The cult of Masonry and New Age is Satanic, and therefore "darkness.'

In addressing the tribes Moses said "Dan is a lion's whelp, he shall leap from Bashan."[226] The tribe of Dan had been assigned the territory west of Benjamin, north of Judah, south of Ephraim. The land extended to the sea and bordered modern Tel Aviv. The tribe of Dan was not able to capture its inheritance. "The Amorites drove the Danites back into the highlands and would not let them come down into the plain,"[227] as did the Philistines.[228] Dan turned its back on its assigned territory and marched northward with 600 warriors and settled in the northern part of Israel at Laish (which means 'lion' and thus the 'lions whelp' of Jacob), at the foot of Mount Hermon on the frontiers of Bashan (which is in Syria). On the road they passed through Ephraim. Five of their scouts entered Micah's house in Ephraim, took his "carved statue, the ephod, the domestic images and the idol cast of metal...(while the 600 men equipped for war remained outside the gate)...and erected them in Laish which they renamed Dan."[229] "So, having taken the god made by Micah, and the priest who had been his, the Danites marched on Laish, on a peaceful and trusting people. They put it to the sword and burned it to the ground. There was no one to come to the rescue since it was a long way from Sidon and had no contact with the Aramaeans."[230] The rider fell off backwards! (Communism and Freemasonry entice the priest with a quest for power).

The priest they took from Micah "...was a young man of Bethlehem in Judah, of the clan of Judah, who was a Levite and resided there as a

74

stranger. He went out from the city of Bethlehem...as he was on his journey he came...into the house of Micah. He was asked by him whence he came. He answered, 'I am a Levite of Bethlehem Judah, and I am going to dwell where I can, and where I can find a place to MY advantage.'"[231] This Levite forsakes his God-given duties in exchange for money and position (Ecclesiastical Masonry) with the authority and power of the 600.

Now we have a picture of the 600 in the 666. The Danites were the only clan who could not take any of the territory of their assigned heritage. They forsook God, and set up their own false gods and false idols. They took infidel priests who would do their wishes for position and vain glory. They were cruel and merciless in their destruction of "a peaceful and trusting people." "From Dan you can hear the snorting of his horses; at the neighing of his stallions the whole country quakes; they are coming to devour the country and its contents, the town and those that live in it. Yes, now I am sending you poisonous snakes against which no charm exists; and they will bite you, the Lord declares."[232] Jesus Christ was betrayed by one who walked with Him. Through Ecclesiastical Masonry, Pope John Paul II will be attacked by a 'friend,' and the false prophet put in his place.

When the people of the world reject Jesus and Christendom, when they choose falsehood and false promises, they leave themselves open to receive the poisonous snakes and will certainly quake at the approaching stallions. The armed warriors of the Antichrist and his New Age Militants will be many, swift and cruel. People will fear them, but the Believers in Jesus Christ will have their trust in Him, and the serpent and his lowly vipers will not bring fear to them. With advancing armies of Heaven, the people **OF** the world will quake because they have forsaken God. The Body of Christ already know that the woman of Genesis 3:15, clothed with the sun of Revelation 12:2 will crush the head of the serpent.

"King Nabuchadnezzar had a golden statue made, 60 cubits high and 6 cubits wide...A herald loudly proclaimed, 'Peoples, nations, languages! Thus are you commanded: the moment you hear the sound of horn, pipe, lyre, zither, harp, bagpipe and every other kind of instrument, you will prostrate yourselves and worship the golden statue set up by King Nabuchadnezzar. Anyone who does not prostrate himself and worship will immediately be thrown into the fiery furnace."[233] In that statue was wrapped up the vain glory of man, the sin and wickedness of man and all the falsehood that existed. The statue denied God. The 60 of the Antichrist, he wanted to be bigger than God. In this modern 1992 generation, how many people, nations and languages prostrate themselves and worship the golden disks of 'modern music?' Did you ever, in front of the youth of

75

today, criticize the music known as 'heavy metal,' 'rap' or such like? Was their reaction passive or angry? The minds of our young are already conditioned to accept the Antichrist.

The number 6 signifies man. God said "Let us make man to Our own image and likeness...and God created man to His own image, to the image of God He created him, male and female He created them...the sixth day."[234]

The man born in this generation wants to be stronger and bigger than God his Creator. Masonic 'New Age' false christ and false church give man that false security.

"Alas for you, Chorazin! Alas for you, Bethsaida!... And as for you Capernaum...DID YOU WANT TO BE RAISED HIGH AS HEAVEN? YOU SHALL BE FLUNG DOWN TO HELL."[235] With the exception of Bethsaida, these towns are in Galilee, the Galilee of Jesus. Bethsaida is in Bashan, in the Golan area, which was Syria, and all three are around the Sea of Galilee, and it is from the genealogy of this area that the Antichrist will come.

"Then I saw a beast emerge from the sea...and the whole world had marvelled and followed the beast...and they prostrated themselves in front of the beast, saying, 'Who can compare with the beast? Who can fight against him?...Then I saw a second beast, emerging from the ground...it was able to lead astray the people of the world and persuade them to put up a statue in honor of the beast...and to have anyone who refused to worship the statue of the beast put to death...anyone clever may interpret the number of the beast; it is the number of a human being, the number 666."[236]

Jesus Christ, true God and true Man, will not leave His flock defenseless. "I saw another angel rising where the sun rises, carrying the seal of the living God...'Wait...until we have put the seal on the foreheads of the servants of our God'...And I heard how many had been sealed, one hundred and forty-four thousand, out of all the tribes of Israel."[237] Twelve thousand were sealed from each of the tribes, except Dan. Dan is not mentioned. Twelve is the sacred number squared and multiplied by one thousand and so the 144,000 represents the totality of the multitude of all of who have been faithful to Christ.

666 has other meanings which our Blessed Mother points out.[238] It is double the number 333 which indicates the divinity of the Triune God.

Satan wants to put himself above God and consequently bears the number 666.

666 indicated once, that is for the first time, expresses the year 666. In THIS PERIOD OF HISTORY Islam was born. Islam directly denies the mystery of the divine Trinity and the divinity of Jesus Christ. The Islamic captivity of Israel (formerly Palestine) was from 640 to 1917. Was 1917 a major attack on 666? Very definitely yes. Fatima proves this.

666 indicated twice, that is for the second time, expresses the year 1332. In THIS PERIOD OF HISTORY the Antichrist is manifested through a radical attack on the faith in the word of God. The kind of agitation fostered by Albigensianism which started in France around 1300 grew. Through the philosophers who gave exclusive value to science and then to reason, there was a gradual tendency to constitute human intelligence alone as the sole criterion of truth. This gave way to the Protestant Reformation in which tradition is rejected and ONLY Sacred Scripture (a portion of it) is accepted, but even this must be interpreted by means of reason. This caused a great division in the Church.

666 indicated thrice, that is for the third time, expresses the year 1998. In THIS PERIOD OF HISTORY Freemasonry assisted by its ecclesiastical form, will succeed in setting up the false christ and the false church. The great revolt will happen and the door will have opened for the appearance of the very person of the Antichrist.

All this does not mean that the Evil One will have everything his own way. No he will not. We must have faith in Jesus. This is why He asked; "'When the Son of Man returns, will He still find faith on earth?'...to prepare you for His second coming and to describe for you a circumstance which will be indicative of the proximity of His glorious return...The spread of apostasy is therefore the sign which indicates that the second coming of Christ is, as of now, close at hand."[239]

"With extraordinary signs which I am giving in every part of the world, through my messages and through my so frequent apparitions, I am pointing out to everyone the approaching of THE GREAT DAY OF THE LORD."[240] "I am the dawn that announces the arrival of THE GREAT DAY OF THE LORD."[241]

Examine this "GREAT DAY OF THE LORD." "Blow ye the trumpet in Sion, sound an alarm in My holy mountain, let all the inhabitants of the land tremble, because the DAY OF THE LORD comes, it is nigh at hand."[242]

"Woe to them that desire the DAY OF THE LORD, to what end is it for you? The DAY OF THE LORD is darkness, and not light. As if a man should flee from the face of a lion, and a bear should meet him; or enter into a house, and lean with his hand upon the wall and a serpent should bite him. Shall not the DAY OF THE LORD be darkness, and not light; and obscurity, and no brightness in it?"[243] The evil and cunning forces of power and monopoly who now seek total control of the earth will shortly have no rest. Present and past rulers and their assistants are being called to account for their past deeds of rulership and mismanagement. "For behold THE DAY shall come kindled as a furnace, and all the proud, and all that do wickedly shall be stubble, and THE DAY that comes shall set them on fire, says the Lord of Hosts, it shall not leave them root, nor branch."[244]

In summary, the Antichrist will be from the tribe of Dan. As Dan was not able to take control of his given territory, so too the Antichrist will not be able to take control of the Church but will accept a false priesthood and set up the false church and false idols. He will be born out of wedlock to a whore in Chorazin, in that he will forsake his habitat and prostitute himself for money and power. He will be brought up in Bethsaida, that is outside Israel. He will have his mind not on the things of the Church, but on his own ambitions. He will begin his rule in Capernaum that is the place where Jesus went after His temptation by Satan. It was from here that he called the first disciples to follow Him. The Antichrist will fail and succumb to temptation and will seduce his first followers, the false prophet and others to come with him and leave the place of their first ministry. Just as the disciples had discussed with one another which of them was the greatest, the Antichrist will set himself up as the 'greatest.' DID YOU WANT TO BE RAISED HIGH AS HEAVEN? YOU SHALL BE FLUNG DOWN TO HELL. The end of the Antichrist is already written.

In everything he does, the Antichrist will try to imitate the physical life of Jesus, but as in Jesus dwells the fullness and goodness of The Godhead, so too in the Antichrist will be the fullness and all the wickedness of the devil. He has set up his satanic trinity, the three frogs. He will have a man traverse the world extolling his greatness. This 'third man' is his "spirit," the false prophet. He will persuade some of the elect, especially those who rebel at authority, to leave the true faith and follow his liberal teachings. He will convince those lacking in knowledge that wrong is right; that he is a merciful god and that our appetites are made for immediate satisfaction. He will try to reverse all law and order upon earth and will fulfill what the scriptures say of him, "The Lawless One." He will require of people only their belief in his divinity, and he will make religion a convenience. He will "deliberately choose the enemies of religion to administer the country."[245] Remember he false currency, now accepted and believed. Remember the reversal of prayer in the school, now accepted and believed. Remember the reversal of God in public schools and places, now accepted and believed. Everything is in place. He has already begun through his many antichrists by having divisions among the brethren. We see too sadly today many different 'church leaders' criticize the Pope and the Church. Is this criticism from The Holy Spirit? Of course not, it is from the evil spirit! We see today many churches rejecting a literal translation of the bible and teaching that faith must pass the test of reason and understanding. Beware of 'convenience' as a fatal substitution for 'lack of faith,' beware of antichrists. "Look to yourselves, that you do not loose what you have worked for, but that you may receive a full reward."[246]

Because of Antichrist's divinations, persuasiveness, wealth and power, the Jews will accept him as the Messiah, and will follow him. He will move his headquarters to Jerusalem and declare it to be his world headquarters. He will call for the dispersed Jews to come home to Israel, promising to rebuild the Temple, in which he will set up his abomination. The Temple will not be rebuilt and this is foretold "...on the wing of the Temple will be the appalling abomination until the end, until the doom assigned to the devastator."[247] The Romans destroyed the Temple in 70 AD. It will remain this way until The New Jerusalem comes out of Heaven.[248] He will reign in terror and horrible brutality for 42 months. Then comes his end, "Though you soar like an eagle, though you set your nest among the stars, I shall bring you down from there! - declares the Lord."[249]

The United Nations, World Bank and International Monetary Fund will be under his control. Just as the nations succumbed to the UN "money power" in 1990, so too the UN, will be the police force for the whole world and as we saw earlier it will also be the New World Order department of law, social reform, and all the other agencies, covert, clandestine and brutal.

"Now, I urge anyone who may read this book not to be dismayed at these calamities, but to reflect that such visitations are intended not to destroy our race but to discipline it."[250] Jesus will send His two prophets, Enoch and Elijah, who will confront the Antichrist face to face, and will challenge him publicly. These two prophets of The Lord Most High have ascended to Heaven where they have been instructed in the Government of God. They will descend to earth in the LAST DAYS to communicate with and encourage the little flock in establishing and running of The Government of God on earth. The Antichrist will kill the two witnesses and will not let them be buried. In fulfillment of the scriptures, God will raise them to life after three and a half days, and in full view (television?) of the whole world He will bring them up to heaven. This will cause a great conversion and return to Jesus Christ.

These three days will be days of darkness for all humanity. As Jesus was in the tomb for three days, so too the world will be in darkness for three days. Just as Saul was toppled from his high horse on the road to Damascus, so too will the world be toppled from its high horse on its road to Damnation. Like Saul, some will ask "Who are You Lord?" and these shall be led away by the hand to a place of refuge. Others will curse the darkness as they go on to Damnation.

During these three days the fury of hell will be unleashed. The enemy will be in a desperate rage, and only those secured in Jesus will survive. As prophesied in Mordecai's dream: "There were cries and noise, thunder and earthquakes, and disorder over the whole earth. Then two great dragons came forward, each ready for the fray, and set up a great roar. At the sound of them every nation made ready to wage war against the nation of the just. A day of darkness and gloom, of affliction and distress, oppression and great disturbance on earth!"[251]

"Go, My people, enter into thy chambers, shut thy doors upon thee, hide thyself a little moment, until the indignation pass away."[252] The faithful remnant are to go into their homes, seal the doors and cover the windows. They are to light blessed bees wax candles and under no circumstances open the door or look outside until the retribution and darkness has passed. We cannot look upon the fury of God and live. The evil spirits will come knocking at our doors and imitate our loved ones and try to convince us to open the door. Do not be deceived. Those on the outside will already be dead. "For behold the Lord will come out of His place, to visit the iniquity of the inhabitant of the earth against him, and the earth shall disclose her blood, and shall cover her slain no more."[253]

There will be a famine over all the earth and after this God shall cut off the food supply. Those who have paid heed to the warnings will survive, those who do not, will offer their heritage for a bowl of stew.[254] The scoffers will send their servants to their wells of supply only to be dismayed at the emptiness therein.[255] They will return to their earthly masters to report that the wells are empty. The earthly masters whom they have served, will accuse them and punish them for negligence, not knowing that The Master has claimed retribution. The stores will be empty, the crops in the fields will be scorched and destroyed, the rulers of injustice and iniquity will be removed. During this time we must pray, pray and "take courage, call on God and He will deliver you from tyranny, from the clutches of your enemies."[256]

Remember that we are not alone, that we have help, and that we will be victorious in Christ. "This is the hour of the Angelic Powers. It is the Angelic Powers who are guiding all my children in the decisive battle for the final defeat of Satan and the coming of the glorious reign of Christ, in the triumph of my Immaculate Heart in the world."[257]

"Seeing it is a just thing with God to repay tribulation to them that trouble you, and to you who are troubled, rest with us when the Lord Jesus shall be revealed from heaven, WITH THE ANGELS OF HIS POWER, in a flame of fire, giving vengeance to them who know not God, and who obey not the gospel of our Lord Jesus Christ. Who shall suffer eternal punishment in destruction, from the face of the Lord, and from the glory of His power, when He shall come to be glorified in His saints, and to be made wonderful in all them who have believed, because our testimony was believed upon you in that day."[258] "It then happened that all over the city for nearly forty days there were apparitions of horsemen galloping through the air in cloth of gold, troops of lancers fully armed, squadrons of cavalry in order of battle, attacks and charges this way and that, a flourish of shields, a forest of pikes, a brandishing of swords, a hurling of missiles, a glittering of the golden accoutrements and armor of all kinds. Wherefore all men prayed that these prodigies might turn to good"[259] So too we pray.

After this the Antichrist and his false prophet will be overpowered, his reign of terror will come to the end and cast down to hell for all eternity. "In the hour of the great trial, paradise will be joined to earth, until the moment when the luminous door will be opened, to cause to descend upon the world the glorious presence of Christ, Who will restore His reign in which divine Will shall be accomplished in a perfect manner, as in heaven, so also on earth."[260]

When the darkness has lifted then God's holy ones who have held His word in their hearts and in their actions with joy and jubilation, to receive their inheritance, the humble shall devour the mighty.[261] It is written that the meek shall inherit the earth and God's people who have persevered to the end will be given the authority which Jesus received from Our Father. To such people He will give the scepter to rule and eliminate the pollution of the physical, the political, the moral and the spiritual. They will rule with a rod of iron and shatter the bonds of deceit and injustice into many potsherds.

Justice will reign under The One Who alone is Justice. Peace will reign under The One Who alone is Peace. Harmony will reign under The One Who alone is Harmony. The breach of dissention will be repaired, the walls of trust will be rebuilt, and the city of God's faithful will be inhabited. Those who are aware and alert will reach out and save those in distress. Those who are prepared will save those who are the prey of the wolves. Those who love Jesus will be good shepherds, they will feed His lambs, and yes, they will feed His sheep. This will cause a great many to leave their unbelieving ways and to convert to Christ. Most Jews and Moslems will become Catholic, as will the whole wide world.

"But unto you that fear My name, the Sun of justice shall arise, and health in his wings, and you shall go forth, and shall leap like calves of the herd. And you shall tread down the wicked when they shall be ashes under the sole of your feet in THE DAY that I do this, says the Lord of Hosts."[262] We may ask if this suffering is necessary and beneficial. Who wants to live with habitual evil? "This is therefore the travail of the new birth. And, as a mother, I am called to the task of begetting today, in suffering, the new humanity, ready for the meeting with its Lord, Who is returning to you in glory."[263]

**THOSE WHO LOOK down WILL SEE The Antichrist;
THOSE WHO LOOK UP WILL SEE CHRIST.**

CHAPTER 10

THE FINAL PREPARATION

"God is tender and compassionate, slow to anger, rich in faithful love, Who relents about inflicting disaster."[264] He is not without His victorious Master Plan. Defeat cannot attack Him. He knows the end from the beginning and has already given us the answer. We are urged to repent and change, "Come out, My people, away from her, so that you do not share in her crimes and have the same plagues to bear."[265] The Roman Catholic Church, the true and full believers, are sealed with "the seal on the foreheads of the servants of our God."[266]

Because of the steadfast love for Jesus by Pope John Paul II, many more are converting to the full word of God, and this includes 'lukewarm' Catholics. The Church is a beacon, just as God has said, "That day, the root of Jesse, standing as a signal for all peoples, will be sought out by the nations and its home will be glorious. When that day comes, the Lord will raise His hand a second time to ransom the remnant of His people, those still left, from Assyria, from Egypt, from Pethros, Cush, and Elam, from Shinar, Hamath, and the islands of the sea. He will hoist a signal for the nations and assemble the outcasts of Israel; He will gather the scattered people of Judah from the four corners of the earth,"[267] "and there will be shelter to give shade from the heat by day, and refuge and protection from the storm and rain."[156]

The "refuge" is where "the woman fled into the wilderness, where she has a place prepared for her by God, that there they may nourish her a thousand two hundred and sixty days." This place of refuge is not designed by human hands, but by God. It is prepared by the Spirit of God. It is a physical place in a physical wilderness protected under God in Mary's Immaculate Heart. A typical example of this place of refuge was seen on the 6th of August 1945 in Hiroshima, Japan. The atomic bomb was dropped only eight short blocks from a house where a German Jesuit priest called Father Hubert Shiffner and seven of his colleagues stayed. Although disaster and lethal destruction raged around them, they escaped without any harm from either radiation or blast. Since that time those eight survivors have been examined by over two hundred scientists to try to understand how they could have escaped unharmed. Speaking on USA television, Father Shiffner gave the startling answer, "In that house the Rosary was prayed every day. In that house we lived the message of Fatima." A

83

Franciscan monastery founded by Saint Maximilian Kolbe escaped similar harm three days later in Nagasaki when the second atomic bomb was dropped. Destruction all around, while the secure refuge remained intact. By the mighty hand of God the faithful were protected in the fiery furnace.[268]

The Church, the faithful remnant, is the woman which fled into the wilderness, that is, ostracized by the majority of 'society', where she (the Church) has a place (of refuge in Mary's Immaculate Heart) prepared for her by God, that there they (the little remnant), may nourish her, (the rest of the Church, that is the "other sheep... that are not of this fold...also I must bring, and they shall hear My voice, and there shall be one fold and one shepherd,")[269] for the duration of the great tribulation. To the remnant God said, "You will build on age-old foundations; and you shall be called 'The Repairer of the breach.'"[6] The Body of Christ will succeed and will not be overcome or run off the face of the earth. The remnant will receive many coming out of the great tribulation, and comfort and instruct them and give them solace.

Those believing in and exercising the full oral and written gifts are part of the "faithful remnant." This body will be "blessed with EVERY spiritual blessing," and His grace will abound beyond measure in them "in all wisdom and prudence so that He may make known to them the mystery of His will according to His good pleasure."[270]

The little flock which follows Jesus Christ and all His teachings is THE BODY OF CHRIST, the faithful remnant. Not all of God's people belong as yet to the Body of Christ nor to the remnant, because there are "other sheep...that are not of this fold." There are still a number on the outside and they are gradually now entering, realizing that "he who is not against you is for you."[271]

Not all who know the Lord keep faith. St. Paul deviated from his usual farewell greetings when instead of invoking the body of Christ he said to Titus, "Greet those who love us in the faith."[272] There were many disciples who knew the Lord, but when He told them about the Eucharist, "many...turned back and no longer went about with Him."[273] Jesus asks, "Where is your faith?"[274] He asks us again, "When the Son of Man comes, will He find, do you think, faith on earth?"[275] We shall deal with faith a little later.

Over the years since the acrimonious days of the Protestant Reformation, the Protestant churches have moved much closer to the Roman Catholic

Church. In many instances they are beginning to accept Second Thessalonians 2:15 and hold on to the written and oral traditions. They are beginning to accept that before the written Bible Jesus said "He that heareth you heareth Me."[276] To emphasize this point Jesus said in the gospels and 7 times in the first 3 chapters of Revelation, "He who has ears let him hear." Today, despite the apostasy by a number of priests, hierarchy and their followers, there are a number of Protestant ministers joining the Catholic Church, and we are happy to see that they are now priests in the Church. We remember with gratitude the words from The Acts of the Apostles "A large number also of the priests accepted the faith."[172]

Members of the Body of Christ will not judge because they realize that Jesus will not come again to be judged, but to judge those who judged Him. Because we are the Body of Christ we will not judge each other, for in doing so we bring condemnation on ourselves. How can we be other than brothers and sisters in the Lord? When hanging from the cross, Jesus said to His Blessed Mother, "Woman, behold your son!" and then He said to John, "Behold your mother!" Jesus said this to us as John was our representative beneath the cross. "Blessed are they who hear the word of God and keep it."[277]

This assignment to all of us of Mary as our mother, and all believers as brothers and sisters to each other, is a further fulfillment of the word "'Who is My mother? Who are My brothers?' And stretching out His hand towards His disciples He said, 'Here are My mother and My brothers. Anyone who does the will of My Father in heaven is My brother and sister and mother.'"[278] Yet we hear people who profess to be Christians "sit there, slandering your own brother, you malign your own mother's son. You do this, and am I to say nothing? Do you think that I am really like you? I charge you, indict you to your face. Think it out, you who forget God, or I will tear you apart without hope of a rescuer."[279]

From the cross Jesus told us to look to our mother. The argument is made by fundamentalists that we should only go directly to Jesus and use no intermediaries and no intercessors. I often wonder about the marriage feast of Cana. Jesus was there, Mary was there. The servants went to Mary. Why? Is it because they knew that she would intercede for them with her Son? Jesus Himself gives us a number of examples in which we use others as intercessors, and I sight here just two. First, in the transfiguration, He was seen talking with Moses and Elijah.[280] Now Moses had died[281] and Elijah was taken up alive into heaven.[282] By this encounter of the living and the dead, Jesus shows us the communion of saints, living and dead. Because this is so He further demonstrates the power of intercessors, "I

85

shall send you the prophet Elijah..."[283] In the second example the rich man looked up from the flames of hell and saw Lazarus in the embrace of Abraham. He said, "Father Abraham, pity me and send Lazarus to dip the tip of his finger in water and cool my tongue..."[284] Jesus taught us about intercessors, and gave us His mother with His last words to us from the cross..."Behold thy mother."[285] The Father gave us Jesus through Mary, what better acknowledgement of the Father than by approaching Him the same way? "Naked I came out of my mother's womb, and naked I shall return thither."[286] This is so by accepting Mary as our Mother.

"And other sheep I have that are not of this fold. Them also must I bring and they shall hear My voice, and there shall be one fold and one shepherd."[269] The war called "Desert Storm" emphasized that Jesus wants souls, not bodies. He is calling for everyone to return to Him with a repentant heart. He is still calling the nations far away, "For I would not brethren, have you ignorant of this mystery, lest you should be wise in your own conceits, that a partial blindness only has befallen Israel, until the full number of the Gentiles should enter, and thus all Israel should be saved."[287] "Amen, Amen I say to you, he who enters not by the door into the sheepfold, but climbs up another way, is a thief and a robber."[288] "And at that time many will fall away and will deliver up one another and hate one another, and many false prophets will arise and will mislead many. And because lawlessness is increased, most peoples love will grow cold."[289] And again Jesus said to the churches "I have this against you...That you have left your first love...to commit acts of immorality...and that you tolerate the woman Jezebel, who calls herself a prophetess and teacher and leads My bond servants astray, so that they commit acts of immorality...and I gave her time to repent; and she does not want to repent of her immorality. Behold I will cast her upon a bed of sickness and those who commit adultery with her into the great tribulation, unless they repent of their deeds."[290]

As we have seen earlier, Henry VIII established the State church, because the Pope would not annul his marriage, would not grant him a divorce, after entreating Pope Leo X (1513-'21), Pope Adrian VI (1522-'23) and finally Pope Clement VII (1523-'34) without success. The Church stood firm on the teaching on divorce. Henry established his church on divorce, on his uncontrolled lust, and gave us a forecast of what the Antichrist will establish in our own age. He divorced Catherine, married Ann Boleyn, and before he went to his eternal judgement had beheaded two of his six wives. His church allowed contraception contrary to God's Law. "Knowing that the children should not be his own, when he (Onan) went into his brother's wife, spilled his seed upon the ground, lest children should be born in his brother's name. And therefore the Lord slew him, because he did a detestable thing."[291] The people of the Old Testament knew that contraception was wrong and remember the words, "Take heed to keep thyself, my son, from all fornication, and beside thy wife never endure to know a crime."[292] The immorality born in that 'state church' has led to the excessive liberalism of today when abortion is looked upon as lightly as contraception and divorce. This is the Jezebel "who calls herself a prophetess and teacher and leads My bond servants astray." Because lawlessness is increased, most peoples love has grown cold. What about that figure on divorces, 50%? Has love grown cold?

Good parents look after their children and provide shelter and comfort for them at all times. As they are growing up the parents watch as the children stumble and fall, they pick up the child with loving kindness and set them on their way. So it is with our Father; He watches as we fall, He picks us up and sets us on our way, and most of all He has provided shelter for us since the beginning of time. He gave us Jesus. Jesus is our Rock in whom we seek shelter...the Rock of Ages. When He fed the 5,000 people in the DESERT He commanded them to sit on the GRASS.[293] He has made provision for us in the future as well, a place of refuge, just as in days past when places of refuge were provided for His faithful. Where is this place of refuge? In docility and humility in Mary's Immaculate Heart, in the Catholic Church. We need this place of refuge because we are living in and shall go through the remainder of the great tribulation.

God has told us that there is to be a great tribulation and that we are to prepare for it. There is a false doctrine being preached today called "the Rapture." Those people who preach, teach and look for the phenomenon called "the Rapture" are misleading and misled. There are all variations of "Rapture" theories, such as 'pre-tribulation,' 'mid-trib' and other 'fractional tribs.' How do these 'false christs' and 'false prophets' answer those whom they have deceived now that we are in the great tribulation? Have they prepared their flock? No, these wolves in sheep's clothing are adulterating the word of God. All who are living will go through the great tribulation, and we are in the great tribulation now. The "Rapture" preachers use a partial verse from Thessalonians to support their claim, "We shall be caught up with them in the clouds to meet the Lord in the air, and so we shall be with the Lord."[294] The Catholic Church does not teach this "Rapture." The Church gives the full teaching which briefly is that Jesus taught that there would be a great tribulation but that it would be shortened for the sake of the elect. This is clear language - the elect would have to go through the tribulation. Shall the gates of hell prevail against the Church? Of course not. "The just shall never be moved, but the wicked shall not dwell on the earth."[295] St. Paul teaches us "Behold I tell you a mystery: we shall all indeed rise, but we shall not all be changed - in a moment, in the twinkling of an eye, at the last trumpet. For the trumpet shall sound, and the dead shall rise incorruptible and we shall be changed."[296] In completing the partial verse above Paul's letter is explicit, "For this we say to you in the word of the Lord, that we who live, WHO SURVIVE UNTIL THE COMING OF THE LORD, shall not precede those who have fallen asleep. For the Lord Himself with cry of command, with voice of archangel, and with trumpet of God will descend from heaven and the dead in Christ will rise up first. Then we who live, who survive, shall be caught up together with them in the clouds to meet the Lord in the air, and so we shall ever be with the Lord."[294] All those living at the last day will not die but undergo change from the physical body to the spiritual body. Those "who survive" will be those who have lived through the great tribulation. We will deal with this change in Chapter 12.

God gave us details about what is to happen. "In my vision, when He broke the sixth seal, there was a violent earthquake and the sun went as black as coarse sackcloth; the moon turned as red as blood all over, and the stars of the sky fell onto the earth like figs dropping from a fig tree when a high wind shakes it; the sky disappeared like a scroll rolling up and all the mountains and islands were shaken from their places."[297] Some of this has already happened. A great storm was known as "Desert Storm!" The clean-up of the oil well fires was estimated to continue for two years until 1993, but in actual fact the last fire was extinguished in November 1991.

God also told Pharaoh what was going to happen; "God has revealed to Pharaoh what He is going to do. Seven years are coming, bringing plenty to the whole of Egypt, but seven years of famine will follow them, when all the plenty in Egypt will be forgotten, and famine will exhaust the land. The famine that will follow will be so very severe that no one will remember the plenty the country used to enjoy. The reason that Pharaoh had the same dream twice is that the event is already determined by God, and God will shortly bring it about."[298]

Throughout history our loving Father has given us instructions on places of refuge. First we have to leave Babylon. "Come out, My people, away from her, so that you do not share in the crimes and have the same plagues to bear."[265] Second we have to repent and come back to Him and enjoy His great love, "If My people who bear My name humble themselves, and pray and seek My presence and turn from their wicked ways, then I will listen from heaven and forgive their sins and restore their country."[198] In other words to enter into these places we have to be penitent. "The hand of our

88

God is over all who seek Him for their protection, but His mighty retribution befalls all those who forsake Him."[299]

In these places which Jesus has prepared for His Church, every need for all His people, spiritual, physical and emotional will be met. Everyday life will be carried on there including commerce, industry, agriculture, education, etc. God's people will know where to come, "When that day comes The Lord will raise His hand a SECOND time and ransom the remnant of His people... Look, I am beckoning to the nations and HOISTING A SIGNAL to the peoples: they will bring your sons in their arms and your daughters will be carried on their shoulders."[300]

These self-sufficient places of refuge will be God's work, authority and prize for His people; "Here is the Lord your God coming with power, His arm maintains His authority, His reward is with Him and His prize PRECEDES Him."[301] They are built according to His wishes, to house His people and according to the numbers He will be bringing in, "For thy deserts and thy desolate places, and the land of thy destruction shall now be too narrow by reason of the inhabitants, and they that swallowed thee up shall be chased far away."[302] They will provide total shelter, "They shall not hunger, nor thirst, neither shall the heat nor the sun strike them, for He that is merciful to them, shall be their Shepherd, and at the fountains of water He shall give them to drink. And I will make all My mountains a way and My paths shall be exalted. Behold these shall come from afar, and behold these from the north and from the sea, and these from the south country...ye mountains give praise with jubilation because the Lord hath comforted His people, and will have mercy on His poor ones."[303]

The place of refuge is the Roman Catholic Church. The Pope is BOTH the spiritual and temporal ruler. He is the one to whom Jesus gave the keys of the Kingdom and who as heir to Saint Peter "shall build a temple to the Lord, and he shall bear the glory, and shall sit, and rule upon his throne; and he shall be a priest upon his throne, and the counsel of peace shall be between them both."[304]

God said He "will be a sanctuary, a stumbling-stone, a Rock to trip up the two houses of Israel; a snare and a trap for the inhabitants of Jerusalem, over which many of them will stumble, fall and be broken..."[305] We saw the two houses of Christianity established by the religious schism of Luther and the political schism of Henry VIII. (Read 1 Kings 12). God further cautions us, "I will provoke you to jealousy of those who are not a nation; I will stir you to anger against a senseless nation."[306] Then Isaiah dares to say, "I was found by those who did not seek Me; I appeared openly to those who made no inquiry of Me." To Israel He says, "All the day long I stretched out My hand to a people unbelieving and contradicting."[307] These people, who are not a nation, will be as little regarded as David was, insignificant, obscure and most of all humble, in Christ. They will joyfully do His work, be persecuted and laughed at. Those who are called will know their mission and will be endowed with all the gifts and manifestations of the Holy Spirit. They will speak, act and think clearly and boldly. They will PROFESS and not PROTEST. They will be ONE BODY working in unison with the voice of THE SUPREME COMMANDER, JESUS. They will not clamor for position or want to know who is the greatest, but will seek His will and His grace at all times. They will know and recognize each other, because of the mighty acting-power of the Holy Spirit within them, just as Peter, James and John recognized Moses and Elijah at the transfiguration.[308]

Jesus, The Messiah, is coming the second time, fulfilling His word, answering the cry, "How much longer, God, will the enemy blaspheme?...Why hold back Your hand, keep Your right hand hidden in the folds of Your robe?"[309] and completing the symbolic act of Moses when he took his hand from his bosom the first time it was diseased, just as the world is today, but when he withdrew it a second time it was restored. Jesus is coming a second time, and just as judgment, retribution and redemption were fulfilled at the second banquet of Esther,[310] so shall judgement, retribution and redemption be fulfilled at the Second Advent of Jesus. The world at large did not accept Jesus when He came before. The unbelieving saw the signs and still did not believe. God showed Moses His way and the people His deeds...they soon forgot, and when He came to save mankind as the prophets had foretold, the learned did not believe Him. They expected someone different and "He had no form or charm to attract us, no beauty to win our hearts; He was despised, the lowest of men, a Man of sorrows, familiar with suffering, One from Whom, as it were, we averted our gaze, despised, for Whom we had no regard. Yet ours was the sufferings He was bearing, ours the suffering He was carrying, while we thought of Him as someone being punished and struck with affliction from God; whereas He was being wounded for our rebellions, crushed because of our guilt; the punishment reconciling us fell on Him, and by His stripes we are healed."[311] He came the first time and the world judged Him. He is coming the second time and He will judge the world.

Those who have studied His Word, who are aware of what is couched in the prophecies about these days which are upon us, must come out of Babylon NOW. What does that mean? Spiritually clean up our act, as the first and urgent request. Seek God with all your heart. We do not have to be good to go to Jesus, we have to go to Jesus to be good. On the night before He died, Jesus prayed that heartfelt glorious prayer, "...eternal life is this: to know You, the only true God, and Jesus Christ Whom You have sent...All I have is Yours and all You have is Mine...keep those You have given Me true to Your Name, so that they may be one like Us...may they all be one, just as, Father, You are in Me and I am in You, so that they may be also one in Us...with Me in them and You in Me may they be so perfected in unity..."[312] Each of us must become one with Jesus. By lining ourselves up totally with Jesus, we will become sealed with Him. We will all be one body with Jesus, the Mystical Body of Christ, we are the body, Jesus is The Head.

During the final collapse of Communism in Russia and China there will be a small window of time in which the "little flock," the "faithful remnant" will be formed to meet the demands of the great tribulation. The final battle is on for the winning of these souls by leaders whom God has chosen to lead His people.

"Look I am coming soon, and My reward is with Me, to repay everyone as their deeds deserve. I am the Alpha and the Omega, the First and the Last, the Beginning and the End. Blessed are those who will have washed their robes clean, so that they will have the right to feed on the tree of life and can come through the gates into the city. Others must stay outside: dogs, fortune-tellers, and the sexually immoral, murderers, idolaters, and everyone of false speech and false life."[313] When that day comes, and it is coming soon, "Your oppressors' children will humbly approach you, at your feet all who despise you will fall addressing you as 'City of the Lord', 'Zion of the Holy One of Israel.'"[54]

CHRIST HAS DIED
CHRIST IS RISEN
CHRIST WILL COME AGAIN!

CHAPTER 11

THE FINAL VICTORY

"Better the end of a speech than the beginning. Better is the patient man than the presumptuous."[314] We have entered into the times spoken of by the prophet Joel when "It shall come to pass after this, I shall pour out My Spirit upon ALL humanity: your sons and your daughters shall prophesy: your old people shall dream dreams, and your young people shall see visions."[158] We have entered into the 'end times.' Today the 'visions' of Mary the mother of Jesus, by the children at Medugorje in Yugoslavia and other places throughout the world bear witness to this. A special note here must be made. Pope Urban VIII (1623-44) said "In cases which concern private revelations, it is better to believe than not to believe, for, if you believe, and it is proven true, you will be happy that you believed, because your Holy Mother asked it. If you believe, and it should be proven false, you will receive all the blessings as if it had been true, because you believed it to be true." In the event the Church declares these visions invalid I will gladly abide and support Her findings.

"You are entering into times when the divine action of the Holy Spirit will become stronger and stronger. In these times, the Holy Spirit has the task of bringing you to the realization of the plan of the Heavenly Father, in the perfect and universal glorification of His Son, Jesus Christ. Thus the Holy Spirit is fulfilling His divine mission of giving full witness to the Son and will lead you to the understanding of the truth, whole and entire."[315]

In the pouring out of Spirit upon all humanity, we have been called to a very definite purpose and that is in the Government of God. This is spoken by the prophet Isaiah "...a Son is given to us, and the Government (of God) is upon His shoulders."[23] This is the same Government which was proclaimed when Jesus said "All power in heaven and on earth has been given to Me...go, therefore, make disciples of all nations..."[316] and this is the same authority which was promised "to him who overcomes, and who keeps My works UNTO THE END, I will give authority over the nations...and I will give him the Morning Star."[35] Those who receive the Morning Star will "do all things without murmuring and questions, so as to be blameless and guileless, children of God without blemish in the midst of a depraved and perverse generation. FOR AMONG THESE YOU SHINE LIKE STARS (morning stars) IN THE WORLD, holding fast the Word of life."[317]

The manifesto for this Government of God is clearly spelled out in the Sermon on the Mount, and those called to service are the meek and humble of heart. Those called to authority have the faith of a mustard seed, and those called to faith have no divisions of heart. "Who shall enter the Lord's tabernacle?"[318] Those with faith have no questions; those who have no faith have no answers. Our Holy Father, Pope John Paul II is the current custodian of the 'keys of the kingdom,' the manifesto of the Government of God. He is the theocratic leader of all the people of this earth, he is God's appointed spiritual and temporal leader.

In one of her messages our Blessed Mother states, "Be light and security for all those who form part of other Christian confessions and point out the harbor into which thy must enter in order to fulfill the will on my Son Jesus: the holy and catholic Church, which has the Pope as its foundation and sure guide. (Jesus being the foundation upon which he is building).

I confirm to you that, after the triumph of my Immaculate Heart, there will remain in these countries of yours (Ireland and Britain), solely this one and only true Church."[319] It is not insignificant that this message was issued from the country in which the modern Antichrist government was established. It is also beautiful to see and feel the heartfelt call to those who are outside the Church.

It is written that "Blessed are the meek, for they shall possess the earth,"[320] and again it is written that "...from the days of John the Baptist until now the Kingdom of Heaven has been enduring violent assault, and the violent have been seizing it by force."[84] Now the violent for Christ shall seize it by the force of the Holy Spirit.

Those who are the called, the chosen and faithful[321] are those who have, like Moses, gone into the wilderness for training; like Elijah have gone to the mountains and rivers in obedience; like Jonah have been carried in another direction, and like the blind man, have the eyes opened. For God's purpose shall stand and the word once spoken shall not return until it has accomplished ALL that it was sent out to do.[322]

In the faithful remnant[323] are those to be found who, like David, will come forth at the appointed time, having already been anointed. Those people in God's favor will have unshakable faith and trust in God. They will have had training beyond all other men, and they will have given up all of their worldly desires to follow Jesus. All will have come through the fire and the flood, and all will have been purified by the refining fire of the Holy Spirit.[324] Nothing will remain of earthly infirmities and, like Joshua, they will come forward to rule the spiritual and temporal in perfect unity.[304]

These shall be a people of special calling. They will have reached out to attain all that God has purposed in their earthly lives. Compare this to THREE steps of Jesus. The FIRST step was His private life in Nazareth, comfortable and secure in His parents' home. He had a mission and went on to the next phase. In the SECOND step, He went into the Jordan and came out to the acclaim of the Father and the Holy Spirit to begin His public ministry. His feats and marvels were proclaimed everywhere so that those around Him wanted to make Him king. He walked away from human agency as He did not come to rule, at that time. He willingly entered into the THIRD step, death and oblivion, to the disappointment and bewilderment of His faithful followers. Little did they know the fulfillment which lay in this third step, for in it He took full hold and authority in the Lordship. These of special calling, the faithful remnant "will be like dew from the Lord, like showers on the grass, which do not depend on human agency and are beyond human control."[325]

Many have already passed the test and it is of these people that leaders in authority will come, of whom the prophet Daniel has written, "many of those that sleep in the dust of the earth, shall awake, some unto life everlasting...BUT THEY THAT ARE LEARNED SHALL SHINE AS THE BRIGHTNESS OF THE FIRMAMENT, AND THEY THAT INSTRUCT MANY TO JUSTICE, AS STARS FOR ALL ETERNITY."[46] The Lord has trained a mighty army, and some will return from the graves "at the resurrection OF the just" for this mighty event, greater than the exodus. Remember, it has happened before that "the tombs were opened, and many bodies of the saints who had fallen asleep arose, and coming forth out of the tombs after His resurrection, they came unto the Holy City, and appeared to many,"[47] just as had been foretold in Isaiah[45] and confirmed by Jesus. "Do not wonder at this, for the hour is coming in which all who are in the tombs shall hear the voice of the Son of God. And they who have done good shall come forth unto resurrection of life, but they who have done evil unto resurrection of judgement." [326]

A great number of people wonder at the Catholic reverence and respect for the dead. And why not? We are going to meet them again in person. This respect is scriptural; "Blessed be he of the Lord, because the same kindness which he showed to the living, he hath kept also to the dead."[327] It is also recorded that "when they found on the dead men...objects dedicated to idols, (they) blessed the ways of the Lord, the Upright Judge Who brings hidden things to light, and gave themselves to prayer, begging that the sin committed might be completely forgiven...For had he not expected the fallen to rise again, it would have been superfluous and foolish to pray for the dead, whereas if he had in view the splendid recompense reserved for those who make a pious end, the thought was holy and devout."[328]

One of the tasks will be to fulfill the prophecy where the Church "fled into the wilderness, where she has a place prepared by God, that THEY may nourish her..."[329] Invited into this place of refuge are those spoken of who have no means of repaying...the homeless, the orphans, the lame, the marginalized, the maligned, the faithful...God's people.[330] Some of these people are already in the great tribulation. The refuge into which they have fled at this moment is the spiritual garden of the Immaculate Heart of Mary, where she is instructing them and nourishing them in the word of her Son, Jesus Christ. Their hearts are the wilderness, their humility is nourishment for Mary, who in turn nourishes them with truth, faith, courage and love. She at all times points to God and, as a perfect mother, never leaves nor abandons any children, be they far away sinners or devout Christians. "During these years I am preparing you, by my motherly action, to receive the Lord Who is coming. This is why I have asked you for the consecration to my Immaculate Heart, to form all of you in that interior docility which is necessary for me in order that I may be able to work in each one of you, bringing you to a profound transformation which should prepare you to receive the Lord worthily. I am the Mother of the Second Advent. I am preparing you for His new coming. I am opening the way to Jesus Who is returning to you in glory. Make level the high hills of pride, of hatred, of violence. Fill in the valleys dug by vices, by passions, by impurity. Clear away the barren soil of sin and of the rejection of God."[331] With this preparation and instruction, these people will be given the authority to act.

Mary was the Mother of the First Advent, so it is understandable that she too is the Mother of the Second Advent. Since the saints must inherit the earth and rule it for Jesus Christ until He returns in glory, then where are we today in relationship to that reign and when it will happen? Let us look to scripture and see where we are at, as for the "when" only the Father knows.[332]

"And I saw an angel coming down from heaven, having the key of the bottomless pit, and a great chain in his hand. And he laid hold of the dragon, the old serpent, which is the devil and Satan, and bound him for a thousand years. And he cast him into the bottomless pit, and shut him up, and set a seal upon him, that he should no more seduce the nations, till the thousand years be finished. AND AFTER THAT HE MUST BE LOOSED A LITTLE TIME.

95

And I saw seats, and there sat upon them, and judgement was given to them, and the souls of them that were beheaded for the testimony of Jesus, and for the word of God, and who had not adored the beast nor his image, nor received his character in their foreheads, or in their hands, and they lived and reigned with Christ a thousand years. The rest of the dead lived not, till the thousand years were finished. This is the first resurrection. Blessed and holy is he that hath part in the first resurrection. In these the second death hath no power, but they shall be priests of God and of Christ and shall reign with Him a thousand years.

And when the thousand years shall be finished, Satan shall be loosed out of his prison, and shall go forth, and seduce the nations, which are over the four quarters of the earth, Gog and Magog, and shall gather them together to battle, the number of whom is as the sand of the sea. And they came upon the breadth of the earth, and encompassed the camp of the saints, and the beloved city. And there came down fire from God out of heaven, and devoured them; and the devil, who seduced them, was cast into the pool of fire and brimstone, where both the beast and the false prophet shall be tormented day and night for ever and ever."[333]

What does this have to do with today, and what is the 1000 years? We hear a lot of talk about 'he millennium.'It is the reign of Christ for a thousand years as spoken of in the Apocalypse. "Millennium" is a fixed word meaning exactly one thousand, whereas a scriptural one thousand, as we have seen, can mean a great number.

There seems to be at least two schools of thought or opinions about the 1,000 years. The first is that it is already over, the second is that it has yet to come. Let me say at the outset that no matter when it was or will be, we must live for Jesus with our whole heart and soul, expecting Him today, yet being prepared to wait another 1000 years.

In my humble opinion, I believe the 1000 years began with the Resurrection, in 33 A.D. At about 1350 A.D. Satan was let loose and is presently gathering the forces of evil together for the final battle of Armageddon. Jesus is preparing His remnant to take authority away from the nations. This little flock will live in total faith, in the Spirit of the living God, and will do all things through Him and with Him and in Him. They will usher in a period of peace, a Eucharistic period in which Christ will reign spiritually in the hearts of humanity. This period began in recent times with the greatest outpouring of the Holy Spirit. This period is the Second Pentecost. This outpouring will increase until all which God has willed is accomplished. During this time the Antichrist will be made known and his reign of terror will be ended with his defeat at Armageddon. At that time Jesus will come on the clouds of heaven with His angels and saints, and then comes the Last Judgement.

Let me give my basis for this opinion. There are some great scholars who hold that the 1000 years represented the period of time starting with the Resurrection and ending in the Last Judgement. That Satan 'was bound' means to them that his power was very much limited by the Passion and Resurrection of Christ. Others make the interpretation that the 1000 years began after the end of the persecutions in Rome, and that the 'first resurrection' is baptism. In the early Church, 30 out of the first 31 Popes were martyred, (by any standards that would count as tribulation and painful birth)! If we count the beginning of the glorious expansion of the Church and spreading the Word to all the earth as beginning of the 'millennium,' that is after those first persecutions, then the period beginning in about 350 A.D. and ending about 1350 would for some, constitute the 1000 years. However, I do not fully accept that rigid time-frame because in Sacred Scriptures Jesus said that the Kingdom of God is 'at hand.'[334] As time moved forward He said it 'is within,' "being asked by the Pharisees, 'When is the Kingdom of God coming?' He answered and said to them, 'The Kingdom of God comes unawares ...For behold, the Kingdom of God is within you.'"[335] He said there are those standing here who will not see death before they see the Kingdom of God.[336] It goes without saying that some of those standing there did see the establishment of the Kingdom of God. Now since it comes 'unawares,' I am not remotely interested in trying to figure out 'when." I must be ready for 'when' now.

The Second Coming is Christ living in us and through us spiritually, with we, His faithful ruling over the earth. The meek shall inherit the earth, establish the Government of God upon the earth and subject all the enemies of God underfoot. They will present Jesus with the fullness of the earth as He intended it to be. The "remnant" is already in place to move when Jesus issues the command.

This reign of 1000 years in my opinion, is the spiritual reign of the acceptance of Christ and ruling spiritually with Him. Through the blood of Jesus we have taken authority over the forces of evil and are empowered to bind them out and cast them into the wilderness. Because we are baptized, 'born again', we are heirs to the Kingdom. At the Resurrection, Christ is the 'first born' FROM the dead. That event truly inaugurated The Kingdom of God. When we are baptized we experience the 'first resurrection'. If we are in the first resurrection we are in the reign of the Kingdom of God. "Blessed and holy is he who has part in this first resurrection...they will be priests of God and Christ and reign with Him a thousand years."

Commenting on the Douay Rheims translation of the Bible is one eminent thinker, Bishop Challoner (1691-1781). In his notes to the Apocalypse he states "that the 1,000 years is for the whole time of the New Testament, but especially from the time of the destruction of Babylon or pagan Rome, till the new efforts of Gog and Magog against the Church, towards the end of the world. During which time the souls of the martyrs and saints live and reign with Christ in heaven, in the 'first resurrection,' which is that of the soul of the life of glory, as the 'second resurrection' will be that of the body, at the day of general judgement."

Satan was let loose at the period beginning with the outbreak of Albigensianism which escalated to the schism by Martin Luther and culminated in the arrival of the mini-antichrist King Henry VIII. Henry gave birth to the modern antichrist government of contraception, divorce and deceit. The faithful have not been conquered, and we are now at the end of the Second Pentecost.

Let me here again invoke the help and enlightenment of our Blessed Mother. She is the heavenly prophetess,[337] and we can believe what she says. To substantiate this claim for example, in 1988 she prophesied, "With Austria and Germany, from here I bless the surrounding countries which are still under the yoke of a great slavery and today I announce that the moment of their liberation is close."[338] This was almost two years before the unexpected fall of the Berlin Wall!

She says, "To me has been entrusted the task of preparing His glorious return."[339] "I am preparing you for His new coming...I urge all humanity to prepare the way for the Lord who is coming. During the last decade of your century, the events which I have foretold to you will have reached their completion."[340] If everything is to be completed, and only a small number of people will remain faithful, then we must strive to be part of that small remnant who remain faithful and "who keeps My works unto the end." The enemies of the Church will be subdued, there is absolutely no doubt about that. God said to Jesus, "Sit Thou at My right hand, until I make Thy enemies Thy footstool."[341] St. Paul says the end comes "when He delivers the Kingdom to God the Father, when He does away with all sovereignty, authority and power. For He must reign, until "He has put all His enemies under His feet."[342]

Moving closer in the understanding of where we are scripturally in relation to all of this, and to putting 'all His enemies under His feet,' an extraordinary event happened about 100 years ago. In our oral tradition we know that in 1889 Pope Leo XIII stopped after Mass and was given a vision of Satan talking to God in which Satan boasted that given 100 years he would conquer all the earth. God granted him his request, knowing that the gates of hell would never prevail against His Church. The good Pope retired to his office and wrote this prayer: "Saint Michael, the Archangel, defend us in the day of battle; be our safeguard against the wickedness and snares of the devil. May God rebuke him, we humbly pray, and do thou O Prince of the heavenly host, by the power of God thrust down to hell Satan and all the wicked spirits, who wander through the world seeking the ruin of souls." The hundred years are over and Satan lost as predicted, but he is still kicking. Jesus conquered death (Satan) at the Resurrection and His Church has reigned for a long time, and because scripture says that "after that he should be let loose for a little while," then the vision of Pope Leo XIII has shown us that we are in the "little while." It is further interesting to note that orthodox Marxism was formed in Russia in 1883 with the organization of a group called "Liberation of Labor." A few years later, Lenin picked up on Marx and began his revolutionary writings in the late 1890's, the writings which became the manual for the communist government of the Red Dragon, Satan.

If we are at the end of the 1,000 years, then the action of all the nations gathered together in battle formation under UN Resolution number 666, and other numbers as previously stated, should be looked at seriously as the ushering in of the period of Armageddon.(The UN is under the control of Communism and Freemasonry). Armageddon will be fought in the area of Megiddo, Israel. Although Israel was not part of the alliance of the nations, Iraq included them by including the 'Palestinian Question'. If all this is so, then two major events have yet to take place, a) the collapse of the system of the world, and b) the great apostasy.

a) The collapse of the financial world and the corrupt governments of the world is through the pouring of the fifth bowl of wrath. This appears to be happening at an accelerated rate. The fifth bowl of wrath was emptied over the throne of the beast and the whole empire was plunged into darkness. The empire of Babylon has oil as one of its strongest bases. If oil is to dry up, industry would come to a halt. In addition to oil shortages, oil spills are causing hardships all over the world, from polluted water to contaminated fish and fowl. When the money dries up God has influenced the minds of Communism and Freemasonry to fight against each other.

b) The other is the revolt, 'the great apostasy,' the great loss of faith.[71] This

99

is the schism which is happening today in the Roman Catholic Church. While there is a conversion of many fallen away back to the true faith of the Catholic Church, there is an element who like 'Dan' want to seize power by deceit.

"The Church, my beloved Daughter, is now emerging from a great trial because the battle between me and my Adversary has been waged, even at her very summit. Satan has attempted to infiltrate to the very point of threatening the rock on which the Church is founded, but I prevented him from doing so.

Precisely when Satan was under the illusion that he had conquered, after God had accepted the sacrifice of Pope Paul VI and of John Paul I, I obtained from God for the Church the Pope who had been prepared and formed by me."[343]

"There has also entered into the Church disunity, division, strife and antagonism. The forces of atheism and masonry, having infiltrated within it, are on the point of breaking up its interior unity and of darkening the splendor of its sanctity. These are the times, foretold by me, when cardinals will be set against cardinals, bishops against bishops, and priests against priests and the flock will be torn to pieces by rapacious wolves, who have found their way in under the clothing of defenseless and meek lambs. Among them there are some who occupy posts of great responsibility and, by means of them, Satan has succeeded in entering and in operating at the very summit of the Church."[344] "The dark conspiracies woven by Masonry, by means of its many followers who have insinuated themselves at the summit of the Church, have succeeded in paralyzing its activity and extinguishing its apostolic ardor."[345]

We have been forewarned to be aware and alert for these antichrists. "For many deceivers have gone forth into the world who do not confess Jesus as the Christ coming in the flesh."[346] Just as the World Council of Churches have denied that Jesus could have said all that is in the gospels, so too this element will herald that heresy. The World Council of Churches is in need of a "leader." When he makes his identity known he will be the false prophet. "Anyone who advances and does not abide in the doctrine of Christ, has not God; he who abides in the doctrine, he has both the Father and the Son. If anyone comes to you and does not bring this doctrine, do not receive him into the house, or say to him, Welcome. For he who says to him, Welcome, is a sharer in his evil works."[346]

Unfortunately a number of priests and hierarchy are mistaking the word of

God which says that Jesus is the same, yesterday, today and forever. Their god has become socialism and they have fallen into the trap of secular humanism. Through false ecumenism they are pandering to the demands of compromise. They are building the idol of a false doctrine, a false church, a false christ. They are building the stage for the arrival of the Antichrist. They have abandoned the teaching of the Pope in favor of their own understanding. God tells us "...lean not on your own understanding,"[347] but these poor unfortunates have joined the serpent in believing his message to Eve "...you will be like God, knowing good and evil."[190] We pray for these and remind them, "Do not imitate evil, but that which is good. He who does what is good is of God; he who does what is evil has not seen God."[348] The false prophet will soon lead those in rebellion against the Pope and the Church out of truth. He will lead them into an already expansive image of the beast, the false church and the false christ.

"As apostles of the last times, you must announce with courage all the truths of the Catholic faith; proclaim the Gospel with force; and resolutely unmask the dangerous heresies which disguise themselves with truth in order to better deceive minds and thus lead astray from the true faith a great number of my children."[349]

We know that there are a lot of trials before us, particularly for our Holy Father Pope John Paul II. "I announce to you that the hour of the great trial is on the point of arriving."[350] "You are entering into the fiercest moments of the struggle and the most painful stage of the great tribulation."[351]

In order to understand this a little bit more fully, let us examine again the two above messages from '79 and '88. "...after God had accepted the sacrifice of Pope Paul VI and of John Paul I..." Pope Paul was steadfast in resisting the pressure of infidels to change God's teachings and compromise to man's desires. He was abandoned and scorned by a number of the hierarchy, clergy and people alike, but he remained faithful and true, offering the sacrifice of his own existence to Jesus. He died a natural death in 1978.

Pope John Paul I was a courageous man and died suddenly after a reign of about 30 days. A seemingly healthy man who would have resisted the demands of the modernist liberals within the summit of the Church. Mary says of him "Love him, listen to him, defend him, follow him, because he will have much to suffer for the Church."[352] She knew before hand that he would only rule for a month. In this context of suffering, I often wonder the meaning of the verse "She brought forth a man child, who was to rule all nations with an iron rod, and her son was taken up to God, and to his

101

throne."[353] Some people argue that this man child was Jesus. It was not. Jesus did not come the first time to rule, but to serve.[354] St. John was "in the spirit on the Lord's day," that is he was in the third heaven. He was told to "write the things which you have seen, and which are, and which must be done hereafter,"[355] but he had already seen Jesus ascend in glory into heaven, not because He might be devoured by the dragon.[356]

The Blessed Virgin Mary is the woman of Revelation 12. Her messages to Father Gobbi are to her "Beloved Sons" of whom the Pope is referred to as 'the first of my beloved sons.'[357] The sudden death of Pope John Paul I marked the beginning of a very painful struggle for the Church with the succeeding Pope John Paul II ardently defending the True Faith against all attackers. We also know that the enemy is angry with the Holy Father and would like him out of the way. Here another verse comes to mind, "Never let anyone deceive you in any way. It cannot happen until the Great Revolt has taken place, and there has appeared the wicked One, the lost One, the Enemy, who raises himself above every so-called God or object of worship to enthrone himself in God's sanctuary and flaunts the claim that he is God...And you know, too, what is still holding him back from appearing before his appointed time. The mystery of iniquity is already at work, but let him who is restraining it once be removed, the wicked One will appear openly."[358] I believe that this restraining power is the Holy Spirit directing our Pope. The Blessed Mother says that "The dark conspiracies woven by Masonry, by means of its many followers who have insinuated themselves at the summit of the Church," and she further says that "I am coming down from heaven, so that the final secrets may be revealed to you and that I may be able thus to prepare you for what, as of now, you must live through, for the purification of the earth. The Church will know the hour of its great apostasy. The man of iniquity will penetrate into its interior and will sit in the very Temple of God, while the little remnant which will remain faithful will be subjected to the greatest trials and persecutions. Humanity will live through the moment of its great chastisement and thus will be made ready to receive the Lord Jesus Who will return to you in glory.[359] Therefore when it says 'let him who is restraining it once be removed' would indicate that the Pope would be violently removed and the Antichrist would appear openly. We must pray continuously for the Pope.

So much for the opinion that we are living in the last period of the 1000 years. What about the opinion that the millennium has yet to come. Here the beliefs are two-fold.

a) Some proponents say that we are living in the imperfect state now and are undergoing purification so that we can arrive at the glorious and

102

perfected IMMACULATE state. This argument is very convincing and I believe it is an interim stage before the Last Judgement. I will deal with this in greater detail in Chapter 12, noting here the IMMACULACY is accurate, however I question the timing. Under this theory the battle of Armageddon would take place after every tear had been wiped away, which I find difficult to accept. I do not discount it, but how do we treat this message, "With a small number of these children, the Lord will soon restore on earth His glorious reign of love, of holiness and of peace."[360] "And you are forming the dwelling place for God among men, that all may become His people, where every tear will be wiped from their eyes and there will no longer be any death, or strife, or mourning, or anguish, because the former things have passed away."[361]

b) Some, mostly Non-Catholic, argue that the Church up until the Protestant Revolt really could not have had the millennium. Treating this thought first, I can easily see where they are coming from. I suppose if I were born into one of the de-nominations I would probably believe that thought too. While I can understand their thinking, I believe that this was the period when Satan was loosed out of his prison, and went forth, and seduced the nations, which are over the four quarters of the earth. My conclusions on this are based on Luther's revolt , which was not the great revolt, but a mini-revolt, compared with what is about to happen. Also Henry VIII brought about the deceitful modern governments as we have seen, and he was a mini-antichrist. The current schism within the Catholic Church is the ground-swell for the great revolt. From the scriptures quoted above from Thessalonianians it appears to me that the Pope must be removed and then comes Armageddon. Also Mary says, "When **this Pope** will have completed the task which Jesus has entrusted to him and I will come down from heaven to receive his sacrifice, all of you will be cloaked in a dense darkness of apostasy, which will then become general."[362]

I believe that the thousand years mentioned six times in Chapter 20 signifies that all man's efforts will be completed before God finally destroys the imperfect. The saints in the last days must reign through Christ, "God, Who is rich in mercy, for His exceeding charity wherewith He loved us even when we were dead in sins, hath quickened us together in Christ, (by Whose grace you are saved), and hath raised us up TOGETHER, and made us sit TOGETHER in the heavenly places THROUGH CHRIST JESUS. That He might show in the ages to come the abundant riches of His grace, in His bounty towards us in Christ Jesus. For by grace you are saved through faith, and not that of yourselves, for it is the gift of God, not of works that no man may glory."[363] The saints must inherit the earth and the promises made to Abraham must be fulfilled. "For not through the law was the promise made to Abraham, or to his seed, that he should be heir of the world, but through the justice of faith."[364] In another place it says "God hath not subjected unto angels the world to come..."[365] This is quite clear that the reign of 1,000 years must take place and Satan (that fallen angel) be put away for all eternity before the final presentation.

"You are preparing to live through the most difficult hours and the greatest sufferings. It is necessary that all of you come as quickly as possible to form part of my army. I am the victorious Woman. In the end, the power of Satan will be destroyed, and I myself will bind him with my chain and I will shut him up within his kingdom of death and of eternal torment, from which he will not be able to get out."[366] "Satan's pride will again be conquered by the humility of little ones, and the Red Dragon will find himself decisively humiliated and defeated when I bind him not by a great chain but by a very frail cord: the holy rosary."[367] The frail cord of the Holy Rosary is the great chain.

It is my opinion that the time for fulfillment of all that we have been waiting for is very close. The events leading up to this moment parallel the events announcing the birth of Jesus and continue all the way to the crowning in Heaven. The events known to Catholics as the Fifteen Mysteries of the Rosary are the events through which some people are and have been going.

The Second Coming has been ANNOUNCED again to some chosen people in a special way. Those who hear and believe are the remnant. It is their duty to relay this message to those who have ears to hear. This proclamation has been made ahead of time to allow them to fully prepare for the sacredness, the sanctity and the magnitude of The Arrival. After the acceptance of this ANNUNCIATION, they have been subjected to AGONIES and trials. These agonies are of different kinds to different people, but each one can relate to what has and is happening in their own personal life. Because of particular commitments given to follow the Morning Star, some have suffered verbal SCOURGINGS of many kinds at the hands of others. Just as the Mother Mary was CROWNED with shame by 'the world' because she was pregnant 'out of wedlock,' many too have been crowned with shame in the womb, in the wound and in the wonder. All who have followed Jesus in this particular call of Morning Star have CARRIED THE CROSS and CRUCIFIED their flesh and their feelings with faith and love in order to complete that which they have been asked to do.

Because they have been faithful to Morning Star, they will soon receive The Divine VISITATION which will bring the good news of the complete Master Plan for the fullness of The Bright Morning Star. Because they have persevered to the end, they will receive the authority which Jesus has received and they shall rule the nations with an iron scepter. This will be the completion of the labor and the fullness of that Plan spoken of so long ago. They will joyfully do the task which Jesus will command and make the PRESENTATION so long awaited to The King of kings. At that time so many will come to the Temple of the Holy Spirit to FIND JESUS.

After the evil one is defeated will come the Judgment and the glorious RESURRECTION of the faithful. These will ASCEND with Jesus into the full glory of eternity and be fully EMERSED IN THE HOLY SPIRIT and so have revealed to them the fullness of The Godhead and the mysteries of creation. With this ASSUMPTION into the Heaven of the heavens, THE CHOSEN PEOPLE will receive that CROWN promised from the beginning.

That marriage feast for which Jesus thirsted on the Cross will be consummated and at that time He shall PRESENT the Kingdom of God into the Hands of Our Father.

Could this be the end? We must be ready and "Expect the Lord, do manfully..and wait for the Lord."[368] In the meantime, we wait, watch and "pray without ceasing. In all things give thanks for this is the will of God in Christ Jesus regarding you all. Do not extinguish the Spirit. Do not despise prophecies. But test all things, hold fast what is good. Keep yourselves from every kind of evil."[369]

The gift of Morning Star is the gift given to us announcing the victory over Satan and the authority given to us by Jesus to reign through Him on earth. This reign is glorified in the 'third heaven,' the new heaven and the new earth.

Jesus is preparing His remnant to take authority over the nations. This little flock will live in total faith, in the Spirit of the living God, and will do all things through Him and with Him and in Him. They will usher in a period of peace, a Eucharistic period in which Christ will reign spiritually in the hearts of humanity.

This period began 1991 with the greatest outpouring of the Holy Spirit in recent times. This period is the Second Pentecost, and this outpouring will increase until all which God has willed is accomplished.

"Begin anew to gather about you the faithful who are entrusted to you, to form with your heavenly Mother a true cenacle of unceasing prayer, which can draw down upon the Church and upon the world the gift of a second Pentecost."[370] Why should we pray for this second Pentecost? Remember the prophet Joel when he prophesied that there would be a great outpouring of the Spirit on all humanity? Well, this is it!

"I am calling upon you to unite your prayer to that of your heavenly Mother, to obtain the great gift of the Second Pentecost. The time of the Second Pentecost has come. The Holy Spirit will come, to establish the glorious reign of Christ and it will be a reign of grace, of love, of justice and of peace. With His divine love, He will open the doors of hearts and illuminate consciences. Every person will see himself in the burning fire of divine Truth. **IT WILL BE LIKE A JUDGEMENT IN MINIATURE.** And then Jesus will bring His glorious reign into the world."[371]

"The spiritual cenacle of my Immaculate Heart is the refuge into which you all must enter in order to receive the gift of the Second Pentecost. Thus, with the powerful weapon of the holy rosary, you will be able to attain again today my greatest victory in the history of the Church and of all humanity."[372] In the book of Job we remember that 'naked I came from my mother's womb and naked shall I return there,' and so for all scripture readers and hearers of the Word, we have this time to show our belief in all that God says and return into the womb, the spiritual womb. The word of God is not a pick and choose agenda, but complete so that not one word is left out.[373]

"The Holy Spirit prepares hearts and souls for the second Coming of Jesus. For this reason, **HE IS TODAY POURING OUT HIS CHARISMS, IN A MANNER WHICH IS EVEN STRONGER AND MORE EXTRAORDINARY THAN AT THE TIME OF THE BEGINNING OF THE CHURCH**. Because you have now entered into the last times, which will lead you to the new era. The task of the Spirit is to prepare humanity for its complete change, to renew the face of creation, to form the new heavens and the new earth."[374]

"Today I announce to you that there is about to be born the new Church of Light, which my Son Jesus is forming for Himself in every part of the earth, so that it will be ready to receive Him, with faith and with joy, in the proximate moment of His second coming. The glorious reign of Christ, which will be established in your midst, with the second coming of Jesus in the world, is close at hand. This is His return in glory. This is His glorious return, to establish His reign in your midst and to bring all humanity, redeemed by His Most Precious Blood, back to the state of His new terrestrial paradise.

THAT WHICH IS BEING PREPARED IS SO GREAT THAT ITS EQUAL HAS NEVER EXISTED SINCE THE CREATION OF THE WORLD.[375]

"Behold the tabernacle of God with men, and He will dwell with them."[376] The adoration due to Jesus truly present in every tabernacle throughout the world is about to be rewarded. "Today I ask all to throw open the doors to Jesus Christ Who is coming. I am the Mother of the Second Advent and the door which is being opened on the new era. This new era will coincide with the greatest triumph of the eucharistic Reign of Jesus.

And it will be the eucharistic Jesus Who will finally give you the gift of the true liberation from every form of physical, spiritual and moral slavery. And thus, in all of you there will shine forth the great dignity of sons of God, created by Him, loved, redeemed, sanctified and saved."[377] We must be totally in love with Jesus truly present in the consecrated host of Holy Communion. We must honor and adore Him in truth and in love. We must believe and open the doors of our hearts to allow the fresh refining breezes of the Holy Spirit to make all things new within us and without of us.

It is in this abandonment into the arms of our Mother Mary which allows us to comprehend more fully the magnitude of the unfolding events. Mary, who in quietness and sereneness said "yes," to the request of the Father, now assists us to say "yes" to receiving Jesus in trust and faith to His request. Say "yes" and awake to ecstatic joy. "In fact, the coming of the glorious reign of Christ will coincide with the greatest splendor of His eucharistic reign among you. The eucharistic Jesus will release all His power of love, which will transform souls, the Church and all humanity.

Thus the Eucharist becomes a sign of Jesus Who, still today, loves you to the end, because He is leading you into the new era of holiness and of grace, toward which you are all journeying, and which will begin at the moment when Jesus will have restored His glorious reign in your midst."[378]

This glorious reign of the eucharistic Jesus among us will be a reign of love, of holiness, of justice and of peace. It will be a time of living the fullness of the mystical body of Christ here on earth, as it was intended. This present time is a time of living the faith, hope and love of God. In trying to get a more complete knowledge of what and how we must study, learn, live, behave, pray and adore God, we must seek the help of Mary.

107

She says, "My Immaculate Heart is the luminous path which leads you to the joyous meeting with Jesus, Who is about to return to you in glory."[379] Unfortunately most people who do not walk that path will miss the great event. In living faith by reason, or a sophisticated religion based on television, they are not in tune with the childish acceptance of the word of God and His heavenly messengers. How many of us can really say what that little teenager said, "Behold the handmaid of the Lord.?"[380]

In this quietness and serenity the full reign of Christ begins to unfold within us. We will hear His voice and His commands. He will show Himself to us more and more until we can see all around us the fullness of His arrival. This Eucharistic Reign will be relatively short. It will grow in intensity among the faithful and will reach its height when we see Jesus coming in the clouds. At that point it will be too late for the obstinate to convert, because He is coming to judge. "HIS SECOND COMING, BELOVED CHILDREN, WILL BE LIKE THE FIRST. As was His birth on this night, so also will be the return of Jesus in glory, before His final coming for the last judgement, the hour of which, is still hidden in the secrets of the Father.

The world will be completely covered in the darkness of the denial of God, of its obstinate rejection of Him and of rebellion against His law of love. The coldness of hatred will still cause the roadways of this world to be deserted. Almost no one will be ready to receive Him.

'When the Son of Man comes, will He still find faith on the earth?' He will come suddenly and the world will not be ready for His coming. He will come for a judgement for which man will find himself unprepared. He will come to establish His kingdom in the world, after having defeated and annihilated His enemies.

Even in His second coming, the Son will come to you through His Mother. As the Word of the Father made use of my virginal womb to come to you, so also will Jesus make use of my Immaculate Heart to come and reign in your midst.

This is the hour of my Immaculate Heart, because the coming of Jesus' glorious reign of love is now in preparation."[381]

"Only this new man, who is born in the paschal mystery of Christ, can throw open wide the door of the sepulchre, in which there lies today the whole of humanity, at this point dead, to cause it to arise to a new era of grace and of holiness, which the risen Christ brought you at the moment of His victory over sin and over death."[382] How many people cannot in humility accept what God is doing and through whom He is working. So many of us have a preconceived idea of what and how God should do things. We have to pray fervently for His Divine Mercy to fall on ourselves and all humanity. Pray for the unity of all people so that not one soul should be lost.[383]

"The great mercy will come to you as a burning fire of love and will be brought by the Holy Spirit...The Holy Spirit will come down as fire, but in a manner different from His first coming: it will be a fire which will burn and transform everything, which will sanctify and renew the earth from its foundations. It will open hearts to a new reality of life and lead all souls to a fullness of holiness and grace."[384]

"Live, in my Immaculate Heart, with the simplicity of little ones, each moment of this new Advent, and make yourselves eagerly ready to throw open the doors of men and nations to Christ Who is coming. And open your hearts to hopefulness, to welcome with joy the announcement which am making to you today: **THE TIME OF HIS GLORIOUS RETURN IS IN THE VERY ACT OF REACHING ITS FULLNESS.**"[385]

We Catholics continuously pray to God for this gift of the Holy Spirit in Psalms "Thou shall send forth Thy Spirit, and they shall be created, and Thou shall renew the face of the earth."[386] "With the Second Pentecost, the Holy Spirit will render His perfect witness to the Son and will bring upon the earth His glorious reign of love, that Jesus Christ may be loved, adored and glorified by a completely renewed humanity."[387] Additionally, Mary asks us to pray a very simple prayer to the Holy Spirit, "Come, Holy Spirit, come by means of the powerful intercession of the Immaculate Heart of Mary, Your well-beloved Spouse." She says, "Let it become your habitual prayer during these years which still separate you from the great JUBILEE of the YEAR 2000, as you live through the concluding times of this second advent.

You are drawing close to the moment when the great prodigy of the Second Pentecost will come to pass.

The Holy Spirit has the task of bringing the Church to its greatest splendor, that it may thus become all beautiful, without stain or wrinkle, in imitation of your heavenly Mother, and be able to spread the light of Christ to all the nations of the earth.

The Holy Spirit has the task of transforming all humanity and of renewing the face of the earth, that it may become a new terrestrial paradise in which God may be possessed, loved and glorified by all.

The Holy Spirit opens and closes the doors of the Second Advent. This is why the entire period of the Second Advent, in which you are living, is the time of the Holy Spirit. You are living in His time.

I urge you to multiply everywhere cenacles of prayer with me. The whole Church must enter into the spiritual cenacle of my Immaculate Heart and recollect itself in incessant prayer with your heavenly Mother, because my Immaculate Heart is the golden door through which the Holy Spirit passes to come to you and to bring you to the Second Pentecost."[388]

What is the significance of the JUBILEE year 2000? "Thou shall sanctify the fiftieth year, and shall proclaim remission to all the inhabitants of thy land...Because it is a jubilee and the fiftieth year."[389] This remission is, according to Challoner, "a general release and discharge from debts and bondage, and a reinstating of every man in his former possessions."

What is this great prodigy? I believe that it is the re-opening to us here on earth of the garden of Eden. God's people will recognize it and have access to it, and will be instructed by those who are now in GLORIFIED FORM. (We will see more about this NEW MAN in the next chapter). This prodigy is the reality that Christ has arrived in His Second Advent. Who can accept it?

"You too are travelling along the last stage of the long journey. You too are coming to the end of the time of the Second Advent. So therefore, live with me and with my spouse, Joseph, the precious hours of this new vigil.

My Immaculate Heart is the bright cave, which brings to an end this Second Advent, because it is with its triumph that Jesus will return to you in glory."[390]

"Live in joy and confidence the last times of this, your Second Advent, by looking to me as to the sign of sure hope and of consolation."[391] The consolation we need will be during the height of the tribulation into which we have arrived. "Let the faith be the only light which enlightens you in these times of great darkness. Let zeal for the glory of God be the only thing which consumes you, in these days of such widespread aridity. You are called to be the new heart of the new Church which Jesus is forming, in a wholly mysterious way, in the heavenly garden of my Immaculate Heart."[392]

Because the time is so short, even by man's standards, we do not have the burden of waiting very long, but we do have the urgency of reaching out with love and kindness to win back souls who are lost and perishing. Some want to hold back and be sure and wait for the moving of the waters,[393] do not be blind, they are moving, do not miss the boat. No one knows the time frame but the Father, and Jesus told us we know the seasons!

"Christ risen is now seated in heaven upon His throne in glory, at the right hand of the Father. To Him all things are subjected. Beneath His footstool all His enemies will be humbled and defeated. As of today, human history is opened up to full glorification of the risen Christ. The risen Christ will come again to you on the clouds of heaven, in the full splendor of His glory. Live today in expectation of His glorious return.

Christ risen is alive in your midst. Christ risen marks with His victory the events of the world and of history. Christ risen wills to restore His Kingdom in your midst, that he may be glorified by the whole created universe. Live always in joy and in a firm hope, in expectation of His glorious return."[394]

When He returns He will join together all that is separated. He will restore us to our loved ones who have participated in the first resurrection. What a joyous moment for we who wait in faith for the GREAT DAY OF THE LORD. "Beloved children, you are sharing today in the joy of the whole celestial and terrestrial Church, which is contemplating your heavenly Mother at the moment of her birth...But yours is like the suffering of a mother who must bring her child to the light. In fact, the immense pain of these last times prepares the birth of a new era, the new times, when Jesus will come in the splendor of His glory and will restore His reign in the world.

Then all creation, set free from the slavery of sin and death, will know the splendor of a second terrestrial paradise, in which God will dwell with you, will wipe away every tear, and there will no longer be day or night, because former things have passed away and your light will be that of the Lamb and of the new Jerusalem come down from heaven upon earth, ready as a bride for her Spouse."[395]

Suddenly it will happen! Jesus arrives on the clouds of heaven with His angels and saints.

"This second coming of His will take place in the light of His divinity, because **JESUS WILL RETURN TO YOU ON THE CLOUDS OF**

HEAVEN, in the splendor of His royalty and will make subject to Himself the peoples and the nations of the earth and all His enemies will be crushed under the throne of His universal dominion.

For this reason, I am manifesting myself today everywhere by means of my numerous apparitions and of my extraordinary manifestations.

My reign of love, which I am establishing in hearts and souls, is the way which prepares the glorious reign of Christ. The triumph of my Immaculate Heart will coincide with the second coming of Jesus in glory, to make all things new.

Open your hearts to hope. The second coming of Christ is near at hand.

Because Jesus Christ, our Redeemer, our Savior and our King, is about to come to you in the splendor of His glorified Body."[396]

"YOU HAVE ENTERED INTO THE LAST TIMES.

And so, receive the prophetic announcements which, in so many ways, have pointed out to you that this, His second Birth, is close at hand."[397]

"Close at hand is the second Pasch in glory. A little while yet and the door of this immense sepulchre, in which lies all humanity, will be opened. Jesus Christ, surrounded by the choir of Angels - on the clouds of heaven prostrate at His feet to form a royal throne - in the splendor of His divinity, will return to bring humanity to a new life, souls to grace and love, the Church to its highest summit of sanctity; and He will thus restore in the world His reign of glory."[398]

When He returns He will give that authority to the little remnant who have remained faithful. They will not have counted the cost, they will not have forsaken the Way. Jesus will know, Mary is at His side interceding for us. "There will remain faithful only that little remnant which, in these years, by accepting my motherly invitation, has let itself be enfolded in the secure refuge of my Immaculate Heart. And it will be this little faithful remnant, prepared and formed by me, that will have the task of receiving Christ, Who will return to you in glory, bringing about in this way the beginning of the new era which awaits you."[399]

"Jesus will return on the clouds of heaven, to restore His reign of glory and to make all things new. Beloved children, live with me today, in expectation of this, His return."[400] With so many of her prophetic

112

announcements already fulfilled, why should anyone want to doubt or delay. How easy and humble it is to kneel at your bedside and say, 'Jesus I behold Your Mother. Mother Mary, help me. Teach me about Morning Star.' These morning stars sing with Jesus. "Thou hast put on praise and beauty and art clothed with light as with a garment."[401] "Where were you when the morning stars praised Me together, and all the sons of men made a joyful melody?"[402]

CHAPTER 12

THE GLORY

Saint Paul was caught up to the THIRD HEAVEN,[403] into paradise, and was taught secret words, which is not granted for man to speak. The Third Heaven has to be understood in terms of scripture and creation from the beginning. Some people have inaccurately interpreted that in heaven there are different levels. That is false. "For this they are wilfully ignorant of, that the heavens were before(1st)...whereby the world that then was, being overflowed with water, perished. But the heavens and the earth which are now(2nd)...are reserved unto fire, against the day of judgment and perdition of the ungodly men...But the day of the Lord shall come as a thief, in which the heavens shall pass away with great violence, and the elements shall be melted with heat, and the earth and works which are in it, shall be burnt up...But we look for a new heavens and a new earth(3rd) according to His promises in which justice dwells."[404]

This world in its present form is passing away, it will end,[405] "(People) shall suddenly die, and they shall be troubled at midnight..."[406] because the Kingdom comes unawares. The scoffers who are trying to bend God to their feeble wills and 'democracy,' "unopposed and numerous though they be, they will be cut down and pass away."[407] When they are taken out of the way we will no longer be seduced by the cunning and craftiness of men (antichrists) in their deceitful scheming.[408] "Amen, I say to you, this generation shall not pass away, till all things be fulfilled. Heaven and earth shall pass away, but My words shall not pass away."[409]

"I saw a new heaven and a new earth. For the first heaven and the first earth was gone, and the sea is now no more."[410] The Third Heaven is the Garden of Eden re-opened, and it is about to be unfolded to us. In order to pass into the garden from this place of exile it is necessary to become fully clothed and perfected, and this means putting on a NEW GARMENT, pure and spotless. "...Be diligent that you may be found before Him IMMACULATE and blameless in peace."[411] For we Catholics, the Sacrament of Confessions is a powerful means of becoming spotless.

The original state of man in the Garden of Eden was a glorified state made in the IMAGE AND LIKENESS OF GOD. "God said, 'Let us make man to Our image and likeness, and let him have dominion over the fishes of the sea, and the fowls of the air, and the beasts, and the whole earth, and every creeping creature that moves upon the earth.'"[168] "They were both

114

naked, to wit, Adam and his wife, and were not ashamed."[412] God gave them a new grace filled garment of original justice.

Man fell from this grace through original sin and consequently the new-grace filled garment of original justice was lost to Adam and Eve, and to all mankind. He saw that he was naked and sewed together fig leaves, and made themselves aprons.[413] This fig-leaf man-made garment is the one which has to be washed clean as we shall see. Man clothed himself in an old garment, this OLD GARMENT is our OLD MAN enslaved to sin.

Adam was expelled from the first heaven. "The Lord sent him out of the paradise of pleasure...and placed before the paradise of pleasure Cherubims, and a flaming sword, turning every way, to keep the way of the tree of life."[414]

Adam begat sons in HIS OWN IMAGE, after HIS OWN IMAGE that is to his own fallen image, which was only a shadow of what God had originally given to him. Here is what Sacred Scripture teaches in regard to the subsequent birth of man. "In the day that God created man, he made him to the likeness of God. He created them male and female and blessed them, and called their name Adam, in the day when they were created. And Adam lived 130 years, and begot a son to his own image and likeness, and called his name Seth."[415] This statement indicates that Seth was born in a "fallen image of God," just as Adam and Eve now had a fallen image and likeness of God, after their sin of disobedience. We are born in the image of Adam, with a soiled, spotted likeness of God, not in that grace filled perfect image and likeness as were our first parents. It is the Sacrament of Baptism that restores us to that grace filled beauty.

Jesus came to make all things new and to restore all things in Himself and to destroy sin and death. He came to clothe us in His NEW GARMENT, His original righteousness, that is in Himself. The garment with which we are clothed is referred to in three particular parables;

THE PARABLE OF THE BRIDEGROOM. "The disciples of John and the Pharisees used to fast, and they came to Him and said, 'Why do the disciples of John and the Pharisees fast, but Thy disciples do not fast?' And Jesus said to them, 'Can the children of the marriage fast, as long as the bridegroom is with them? As long as they have the bridegroom with them they cannot fast. But the days will come, when the bridegroom shall be taken away from them, and then they shall fast in those days.'"

THE PARABLE OF THE OLD AND NEW GARMENTS. "No man SEWS

a piece of raw cloth to an old garment, otherwise the new piece takes away from the old, and there is made a greater rent."[416]

THE PARABLE OF THE OLD AND NEW WINESKINS. "No man puts new wine into old wineskins, otherwise the wine will burst the wineskins, and both the wine will be spilled and the wineskins will be lost. But new wine must be put into new wineskins, and both are preserved. And no one after drinking old, has presently a mind to new, for he says, 'The old is better.'"[417]

Remember Jesus says "No one sews." The first sewing took place in paradise. The fig leaves were used to make an apron as an exterior garment to hide their shame and nakedness. The OLD GARMENT and the OLD WINESKIN is man's fallen nature, soiled and stained by original sin, with it's consequent concupiscenses of the eyes, of the flesh and the pride of life. "For all that is in the world, is the concupiscence of the flesh, and the concupiscence of the eyes, and the pride of life, which is not of the Father, but is of the world."[418] This is the loss of the perfect image of God, that Adam and Eve possessed before their sin. Their original image was lost, never to be passed on to humanity except through Baptism. Ever since then no man has been born in this image and likeness of God, other than Christ Jesus and His IMMACULATE Mother.

THE NEW GARMENT IS THE NEW MAN, clothed in the righteousness of the saints, and the IMMACULATE IMAGE OF CHRIST JESUS.

The New Garments are spiritual garments: 'the righteousness of the Saints,' as the text of the marriage feast of the Lamb link the two parables together. "I heard as it were the voice of a great multitude, and as the voice of many waters, and as the voice of great thunders, saying, 'Alleluia: For the Lord our God the Almighty hath reigned. Let us be glad and rejoice, and give glory to Him; for the MARRIAGE FEAST OF THE LAMB IS COME, AND HIS BRIDE HAS PREPARED HERSELF. And it is granted to her that she should clothe herself with fine linen, glittering and white. For the fine linen are the justifications of the saints.'"[419] When the Bridegroom returns the fast will be over.

The Bride is at this time in Heaven, clothed in her New Wedding Garment, ready to come down to earth and reign in her beauty so "That He might present it to Himself a Glorious Church, not having spot or wrinkle, or any such thing, but that it should be holy and IMMACULATE."[420]

This immaculacy is not an outward facade, it is inner and spiritual. St.

116

Peter makes a clear distinction between the outward and inward clothing. "Whose adorning let it not be the OUTWARD PLAITING of the hair, or the wearing of gold, or the putting on of apparel, but the HIDDEN man of the heart in the INCORRUPTIBILITY of a quiet and meek spirit, which is rich in the sight of God."[421] The Greek word for 'incorruptibility' takes this passage out of the present era, and points to a state when incorruption is restored to the Church, in a new era, because St. Peter is talking about "an inheritance incorruptible, and undefiled, that cannot fade, reserved in heaven for you, who, by the power of God, are kept by faith unto salvation, ready to be revealed in the last time."[422] This inheritance is for us and we must make sure we do not do anything to cause us to loose it.

It is clear from Sacred Scriptures that the OLD GARMENTS are our old man of sin, enslave to concupiscence and the NEW GARMENTS make us totally new creatures, spotless and holy. "As by one man sin entered into this world, and by sin death, and so death passed upon all men, in whom all have sinned...and where sin abounded, grace did more abound. That as sin has reigned to death, so also grace might reign by justice unto life everlasting through Jesus Christ our Lord."[423] That St. Paul is looking towards the future is clear because "...God, Who quickens the dead, and calls those things that are not, as those that are,"[424] thus prophesying future events. So he says, "Knowing this, that our old man is crucified with Him, that the body of sin may be destroyed, to the end that we may serve sin no longer. For he that is dead is justified from sin...Let not sin therefore reign in your mortal body, so as to obey the lusts thereof."[425] But we still do obey it's lusts, sin still reigns in our body, and we still have lusts of the eyes and the flesh and the pride of life. Paul continues, "For sin shall not have dominion over you...But now being made free from sin, and become servants of God."[426]

Happy the man who can apply St. Paul's teaching to himself, and say that his body of sin has been crucified and destroyed so that he no longer serves sin, that he dose not obey his lusts of the eyes and flesh, that he has no pride, that he is dead to sin.

St. Paul continues describing the effects of original sin within himself: "...I am carnal, sold under sin. For that which I work, I understand not. For I do that good which I will, but the evil which I hate, that I do...Now then it is no more I that do it, but sin that dwells in me. For I know that there dwells not in me, that is to say, in my flesh that which is good...But I see another law in my members, fighting against the law of my mind, and captivating me in the law of sin, that is in my members. Unhappy man that I am, Who shall deliver me from the body of this death? The grace of

God, by Jesus Christ our Lord. Therefore, I myself, with the mind to serve the law of God, but with the flesh the law of sin."[427]

He is saying that he still has the 'old man' in him, he is still in captivity to sin, sin dwells and wars in his body. Likewise, he affirms that he has not yet attained the perfect state,[428] and being as great a prophet as he is apostle, he does tell us what will eventually come to the Church to all who obey the Gospel of Glory of Christ when this mystery is revealed. There are many other Scriptural texts in support of this truth. Symbolic of putting off OLD GARMENTS and putting on NEW GARMENTS, and at the same time linked with the Gospel teaching of Jesus, and in Ephesians, Paul is writing about those who refuse the Gospel, alienating themselves from the life of God through hard heartedness, and giving themselves up to all licentiousness, uncleanness, and greediness: "But you have not so learned Christ, if so be that you have heard Him and have been taught in Him as the truth is in Jesus: to put off, according to former conversation, the old man, who is corrupted according to the desire of error {remember Adam & Eve}. And be renewed in the spirit of your minds, and PUT ON THE NEW MAN, who according to God is created in justice and holiness of truth."[429] As long then as mankind is infected with and partakes of the consequences of original sin, mankind (WE) retain the OLD MAN. This is why today we see so many being led away by pride and the false promise of easy living.

Only in the new creation, in the mystery Jesus' Second Coming, do great Saints get the transformation into the NEW MAN, the perfect image of Christ Jesus. St. Paul states that he is the Preacher, Teacher and Apostle of the Epiphania, (an essential aspect of the Second Coming), one must read him in that mystery in order to understand and interpret his writings. Read again the above quotation. The NEW MAN is the new creation, a total putting off of the concupiscence of the eyes, flesh and pride of life. It is the putting off of all sin and the deceits of the devil. It is a totally purified man - body and soul - the whole man! "When Christ shall appear, Who is your life, then you also shall appear with Him in glory. Mortify therefore your members which are upon earth, fornication, uncleanness, lust, evil concupiscence, and covetousness, which is the service of idols. For which things the wrath of God comes upon the children of unbelief...Lie not to one another, stripping yourselves of the old man with his deeds, and putting on the new, him who is renewed unto knowledge, according to the IMAGE OF HIM WHO CREATED him...Put ye on therefore, as the elect of God, holy and beloved, the bowels of mercy, kindness, humility, modesty (gentleness) and patience, bearing with one another, and forgiving one another, if any have complaint against another even as the Lord has forgiven you, so do you also. But above all these things have charity(love), which is the bond of perfection.[430]

We will be clothed with an eternal dwelling out of heaven and our earthly body will be destroyed. "For we know, if our earthly house of this habitation be dissolved, that we have a building of God, a house not made with hands, eternal in heaven. For in this also we groan, desiring to be clothed upon with our habitation that is from heaven. Because when we are clothed, yet so that WE WILL BE FOUND, NOT NAKED. For we also, who are in this tabernacle, do groan, being burdened, because we would not be unclothed, but clothed upon, that that which is mortal may be swallowed up by life."[431] Note here: the TRANSFIGURATION of those who were ready and prepared, has taken place. To understand this one has to recall what Jesus says: "At then they shall see the Son of Man coming in a cloud, with great power and majesty. But when these things begin to come to pass, look up, and lift up your heads, because your redemption is at hand."[432] This is not the redemption of our souls, but of our bodies. St. Paul clarifies this, "But we all beholding the glory of the Lord with open face, are transformed into the same image from glory to glory, as by the Spirit of the Lord."[433] Remember that St. Paul, speaking of the Resurrection of Christ and of our resurrection says, "The first man Adam was made into a living soul; the last Adam into a quickening spirit,"[434] (that is a life giving spirit). When it says 'so that we will be found, not naked,' then we know we must return to our Mother's womb, the Immaculate Heart of the Blessed Virgin Mary.

We must understand the importance of listening to and accepting the Gospel of the Glory of Christ, when it is given to the church by Bishops and Priests united with the Pope, for the Gospel message will come with infallibility. So St. Paul continues his teaching. "And if our gospel be also hid, it is hid to them that are lost, in whom the god of this world has blinded the minds of unbelievers, that THE LIGHT OF THE GOSPEL OF THE GLORY OF CHRIST, WHO IS THE IMAGE OF GOD, should not shine upon them."[435]

God is 'preparing us,' "Now He that maketh us for this very thing, is God, Who has given us the pledge of the Spirit...But we are confident, and have a good will to be absent rather from the body, and to be present with the Lord. And therefore we labor, whether absent or present, to please Him. For we must all be manifested before the judgment seat of Christ, that everyone may receive the proper things of the body, according as he has done, whether it be good or evil."[436] Then comes the NEW CREATION, "If then any be in Christ a NEW CREATURE, the OLD things are passed away, behold all things are made new."[437] Now to take this NEW CREATION and the passing of the OLD out of the 'manifestation of the judgement seat of Christ' and placing it in an era after the time of Jesus' act of Redemption on Calvary, is to loose sight of the mystery of the Second Coming of Jesus which Paul is gradually unfolding.

Incorruption and Immortality are essential to Paul's teaching of the NEW MAN. He has much to say about our resurrection, "For by a man came death, and by a Man the resurrection of the dead. And as in Adam all die, so also in Christ all shall be made alive. But every one in his own order; the firstfruits Christ, then they that are of Christ, who have believed in His coming. Afterwards the end, when He shall have delivered up the kingdom to God and the Father, when He shall have brought to nought all principality, and power, and virtue."[438]

"So also is the resurrection of the dead. It is sown in corruption, it shall rise in incorruption. It is sown in dishonor, it shall rise in glory. It is sown in weakness, it shall rise in power. It is sown a natural body, it shall rise a spiritual body. If there be a natural body, there is also a spiritual body, as it is written: 'The first man Adam was made a living soul,' the last Adam into a quickening spirit! Yet that was not first which is spiritual, but that which is natural; afterwards that which is spiritual. The first man was of the earth, earthly, the second Man, from heaven, heavenly. Such as is earthly, such also are the earthly; and such as is the heavenly, such also are they of the heavenly. Therefore as we have borne the image of the earthly, let us also bear the image of the heavenly. Now this I say, brethren, that flesh and blood cannot possess the kingdom of God, neither shall corruption possess the incorruption. Behold, I tell you a mystery. We shall all indeed rise again, but we shall not all be changed. In a moment, in the twinkling of an eye, at the last trumpet; for the trumpet shall sound, the dead shall rise again incorruptible, and we shall be changed. For this corruptible must put on incorruption, and this mortal must put on immortality. And when this mortal has put on immortality, then shall come to pass the saying that is written: 'Death is swallowed up in victory.' "O death, where is your victory? O death, where is your sting? Now the sting of death is sin, and the power of sin is the law. But thanks be to God, who has given us the victory through our Lord Jesus Christ."[439]

Jesus says in the parable, "No one puts a piece of raw cloth on an old garment. For it takes away the fullness thereof from the garment, and there is made a greater rent."[440] The NEW is not a patch, or a piece, it is the whole NEW GARMENT, and in no way partaking of sin and concupiscence. In no way can it be given without the old man of sin being

120

totally destroyed, crucified, dead wholly and entirely to sin. This FULLNESS that is to come, as Jesus expresses in the parable, is the FULLNESS that St. Paul writes about. There is one Gospel of Christ. Paul's Gospel is his and at the same time Christ's. Christ Jesus has revealed these mysteries of the Gospel to St. Paul when He brought him up to the third heaven, and in visions and revelations. They harmonize perfectly with John's Revelations. "I give you to understand, brethren, that the gospel that was preached by me is not according to man. For neither did I receive it from man, nor did I learn it; but by revelation from Jesus Christ."[441] Paul told us of visions and revelations of the Lord and secret words, which were not granted for man to utter.[403]

WHAT IS THIS FULLNESS?
a) The fullness dwelt in Christ. "(He) is the image of the invisible God, the firstborn of every creature. For in Him were all things were created in heaven and on earth, visible and invisible, whether thrones or dominations, or principalities or powers; all things were created by Him and in Him. And He is before all, and by Him all things consist. And He is the head of the body, the church; Who is the beginning, the firstborn from the dead, that in all things He may hold primacy, because in Him, it has well pleased the Father, that all FULLNESS should dwell."[442]
b) It is the FULLNESS of the Godhead. "For in Him (Christ) dwells the FULLNESS of the Godhead bodily."[443]
c) All the co-sharers in the spiritual circumcision, who co-suffer, who are co-crucified with their passions and lusts, who co-die, are co-buried, co-rise, are co-quickened with Him, receive the FULLNESS of God. "And you are FILLED in Him, Who is the head of all principality and power, in Whom also you are circumcised with a circumcision not made by hand, in despoiling of the body of the flesh, but in the circumcision of Christ (this has not yet occurred but is reserved for the future). Buried with Him in Baptism, in Whom also you are risen again by the faith of the operation of God, Who has raised Him up from the dead."[444]
d) "(I pray)...that He would grant you, according to the riches of His glory, to be strengthened by His Spirit with might unto the inner man, that Christ may dwell by faith in your hearts, that being rooted and founded in charity, you may be able to comprehend, with all the saints, what is the breadth and length and height and depth, to know also the charity of Christ which surpasses all knowledge, that you may be FILLED unto all the FULLNESS OF GOD."[445]
e)"For the perfecting of the saints, for the work of the ministry, for edifying of the body of Christ, until we all meet into the unity of faith, and of the knowledge of the son of God, unto a perfect man, unto the measure of the age of the FULLNESS OF CHRIST. That henceforth we be no more

121

children..."[446] (We are only infants in Christianity in this present era).

This 'fullness of grace' is so unspeakably great that God cannot entrust us with it in our present state of sin and concupiscence. A worse rent would be made in our garment. The garment cannot be old and new at the same time. It is one or the other. Much of the doctrine of St. Peter's two letters explain the doctrine of Jesus in His parables. "As all things of His divine POWER which appertain to life and godliness, are given us, through the knowledge of Him Who has CALLED us by His own proper glory and virtue. By Whom He has given us most great and precious PROMISES, that by these you may be made partakers of the divine nature, flying the corruption of that concupiscence which is in the world ."[447] POWER, Christ has not yet come in POWER. The term CALL refers to the Second Coming. The word PROMISE requires examination. Can anyone in our present state maintain that we are sharers in the divine nature so much that we escape the corruption of the lusts of the world? Are we immaculate and incorruptible?

A time will come when through suffering and a marvelous gift of the Holy Spirit that we will have a total cleansing from all sin, a total freedom from all concupiscence of the flesh, eyes and pride of life, which will occur just before we pass from this war-torn, corrupt world into the new heavens and the new earth. "Therefore, brethren, strive even more by good works to make your calling and election sure. For if you do this, you will not fall into sin at any time. Indeed in this way will be amply provided for you the entrance into the everlasting kingdom of our Lord and Savior Jesus Christ." Paul also says "But we have this treasure in earthen vessels, that the excellency may be of THE POWER OF GOD, and not of us."[448] This 'treasure' is our 'TRANSFIGURATION INTO THE IMAGE OF CHRIST' spoken in "...beholding the glory of the Lord with open face, are transformed into the same image from glory to glory, as by the Spirit of the Lord."[433]

Christians at this time must pray and continue to watch and suffer, until they are confirmed in grace, as St Peter writes, "The God of all grace, Who has called us unto His eternal glory in Christ Jesus, after you have suffered a little, will Himself perfect you, and confirm you, and establish you. To Him be glory and empire for ever and ever. Amen."[449]

If one turns back, as did Lot's wife, and does not flee from the abomination of desolation, "in whom the god of this world has blinded the minds of unbelievers, that the light of the gospel of the glory of Christ, who is the image of God, should not shine on them,"[450] and is caught again in concupiscence, then his last state is worse than the first state of the old man. "For if, flying from the pollution of the world, through the knowledge of our Lord and Savior Jesus Christ, they again be entangled in them and overcome, their LATTER STATE IS BECOME UNTO THEM WORSE THAN THE FORMER. For it had been better for them not to have known the way of justice, than after they have known it, to turn back from that holy commandment which was delivered to them. For, if they do go back the proverb holds true for them, 'The dog is returned to his own vomit, and the sow that was washed, to her wallowing in the mire."[451]

The Lord issues a strong warning. "Be watchful and strengthen the things that remain, which are ready to die."
The Lord issues a strong rebuke. "For I find not thy works full before My God. Have in mind therefore in what manner thou has received and heard, and observe and do penance. If then thou shall not watch, I will come to thee as a thief, and thou shalt not know at what hour I will come to thee."
The Lord issues a beautiful promise. "But thou hast a few names in Sardis, which have not defiled their GARMENTS, and they shall walk with Me in WHITE (garments), because they are worthy. He that shall overcome, shall thus be clothed in WHITE GARMENTS, and I shall not blot out his name out of the book of life, and I will confess his name before My Father, and before His angels."[452] This blotting out is the loosing of the inheritance.
The Lord issues a counsel. "I counsel thee to buy of Me gold fire tried, that thou may be made rich; and may be clothed in WHITE GARMENTS, and that the shame of thy nakedness may not appear; and anoint thy eyes with eyesalve, that thou may see."[453] Forget not the quote from Proverbs, "My son, neglect not the discipline of the Lord, neither be thou wearied when thou art rebuked by Him. For whom the Lord loveth, He chastiseth, and He scourgeth every son whom He receiveth."[454]

"I saw from the mouth of the dragon, and from the mouth of the beast, and from the mouth of the false prophet, three unclean spirits that looked like frogs. For they are spirits of devils working signs, and they go forth unto the kings of the whole earth, to gather them to the battle against the great day of Almighty God. Behold, I come as a thief. Blessed is he that watcheth and keeps his GARMENTS, lest he walk naked, and they see his shame. And He shall gather them together into a place, which in Hebrew is called Armageddon."[455] The Blessed Virgin Mary gives us five stones with which to fight our Goliath. 1. Pray the Rosary. 2. Receive worthily the Eucharist. 3. Read the Bible. 4. Fast. 5. Monthly Confessions. "After these things I heard as it were the voice of much people in heaven, saying: 'Alleluia. Salvation, and glory, and power is to our God. For true and just are His judgments, Who hath judged the great harlot which corrupted the earth with her fornication, and hath revenged the blood of His servants at her hands.' And again they said: 'Alleluia.' And her smoke ascendeth for ever and ever."[333]

Then comes the MARRIAGE FEAST OF THE LAMB. The entry into THE THIRD HEAVEN is achieved through the change of garment. This garment is our glorious perfected state. Then shall the words of prophecy be fulfilled, "...the works that I shall do, he shall do, AND GREATER THAN THESE SHALL HE DO."[456] We certainly have a great gift in store for us, one that I consider the ONLY ONE worth working for here on this earth.

Are you ready? Have you honestly asked Jesus for help? Have you in humility asked the intercession of Mary, the Humble One? Do so now. For what it is worth, I have asked Jesus, Mary and Joseph to bless all who as much as see or hear or read this book and to bring them safely "Home."

In the faith with which I have been gifted, the point of view of this ordinary, quiet and private Irish Catholic has been stated. I may not be everything I am supposed to be, nor what others want me to be. In their eyes I am loaded with faults and shortcomings. I admit all that and even more than my detractors state. In all humility I thank God for His gift of the Sacrament of Confessions through which He has forgiven me my sins. I pray for the gift of being able to get up one more time than I fall down. The cardinal virtues of the Irish are Faith and Fortitude, to betray these are to betray a noble heritage, and so with faith I pray for the strength to keep getting up. "I know how to live humbly and I know how to live in abundance (I have been schooled to every place and every condition), to be filled and to be hungry, to have abundance and to suffer want."[457] With all my faults, I still have ears to hear and sometimes I hear from the pulpits things contrary to what the Church teaches. "There were false prophets also among the people, just as among you there will be lying teachers who will bring in destructive sects. They even disown the Lord Who bought them, thus bringing upon themselves swift destruction. And many will follow their wanton conduct, and because of them the way of truth will be maligned. And out of greed they will with deceitful words use you for their gain. Their condemnation, passed of old, is not made void, and their destruction does not slumber."[458] "For there are also many disobedient, vain babblers and deceivers, especially those of the circumcision. These must be rebuked, for they upset whole households, teaching things that they ought not, for the sake of base gain. For the clean all things are clean, but for the defiled and unbelieving nothing is clean, for both their minds and their consciences are defiled. They profess to know God, but by their works they disown Him, being abominable and unbelieving and worthless

124

for any good work."[459] Eloquence is sometimes to be found in the silence of the pews, not in the verbose demagoguery of the pulpit, yet we know good example is still the best sermon. We may be silent, and we remember to "avoid foolish and ignorant controversies, knowing that they breed quarrels."[460] Unfortunately a number of the leaders of the rebellion against the Church are priests and nuns. They have substituted reason for faith, compromise for fortitude, vainglory for humility, democracy for theocracy, instant pleasure for temperance, and power for piety. In short they are wimps running with the mob who have forgotten the God of their fathers. I pray for you and invite you to "return to the stronghold, you prisoners of hope."[461]

I still believe that being a true Christian is the highest order to which any human being can achieve here on earth, and that being a true Catholic is the highest order of Christianity. Some people ask me what is my "denomination?" I am not de-nominated. I am nominated by God as are all true Catholics. I reject being called a de-nomination.

With joy in my heart I bless all who have had the patience to read these lines with me. If you agree with me, say a rosary for me. If you disagree, say two rosaries for me. If you do not know how, I will send you a free rosary and scriptural instructions. "To Him Who can keep you from falling and bring you safe to His glorious presence, innocent and joyful, to the only God, our Savior, through Jesus Christ our Lord, be glory, majesty, authority, and power, before all ages, now and for ever."[462] In the peace of Jesus Christ I bless you and remind you of an old Irish prophecy:

"They will tax the pigs and goats,
they will tax the ducks and hens
They would tax the very Devil,
should he come out of Hell."

They may not have taxed Granny's hens, but they sure have been making up for it ever since! While we render to God and Caesar, we know that Caesar will have to render to God...and soon.

SELECT BIBLIOGRAPHY

The Holy Bible, The Douay Version, P.J. Kenedy & Sons, New York. 1950.

The New Jerusalem Bible, Doubleday & Company, New York. 1985.

Gary Allen, "None Dare Call It Conspiracy," Concord Press, Seal Beach, Calif. 1971. Available from CPA Books, P.O.Box 596, Boring, OR. 97009.

Father Robert Bradley, S.J. "The Masonic Movement and The Fatima Message," Tape form a conference in Washington, D.C. July 1990.

St. Louis De Montfort, "The Secret of the Rosary," TAN Books and Publishers, Inc., Rockford, IL 61105. 1987.

A. Ralph Epperson, "The New World Order," Publius Press, Tucson, AZ. 85730. 1991.

Fathers Farrell and Kosiki, "The Spirit and the Bride Say 'Come!'" AMI Press, Mountain View Road, Asbury, NJ 08802. 1984

Paul A. Fisher, "Behind The Lodge Door," Shield Publishing Inc., Bowie, MD. 1988.

Father Stefano Gobbi, "To The Priests, Our Lady's Beloved Sons," St. Francis, Maine.

Father Henry G. Graham, "Where we got the Bible," TAN Books and Publishers, Inc., Rockford, IL 61105. 1987.

Father John A. Hardon, S.J., "Modern Catholic Dictionary," Doubleday and Company, Garden City, New York. 1980.

New Catholic Encyclopedia, Catholic University of America, Washington, D.C. 1967.

THE BOOKS OF THE BIBLE IN ALPHABETICAL
ORDER OF ABBREVIATIONS

Ac	Acts	1K	1 Kings
Am	Amos	2K	2 Kings
Ba	Baruch	La	Lamentations
1Ch	1 Chronicles	Lv	Leviticus
2Ch	2 Chronicles	Lk	Luke
Col	Colossians	1M	1 Maccabees
1Co	1 Corinthians	2M	2 Maccabees
2Co	2 Corinthians	Mal	Malachi
Dn	Daniel	Mk	Mark
Dt	Deuteronomy	Mt	Matthew
Ec	Ecclesiastes	Mi	Micah
Ep	Ephesians	Na	Nahum
Es	Esther	Ne	Nehemiah
Ex	Exodus	Nu	Numbers
Ezk	Ezekiel	Obd	Obadiah
Ezr	Ezra	1P	1 Peter
Ga	Galatians	2P	2 Peter
Gn	Genesis	Phm	Philemon
Hab	Habakkuk	Phil	Philippians
Hg	Haggai	Pr	Proverbs
Heb	Hebrews	Ps	Psalms
Ho	Hosea	Re	Revelation(Apocalypse)
Is	Isaiah	Rm	Romans
Jm	James	Rt	Ruth
Jr	Jeremiah	1S	1 Samuel
Jb	Job	2S	2 Samuel
Jl	Joel	Si	Sirac (Ecclesiasticus)
Jn	John	Sg	Songs (Canticles)
1Jn	I John	1Th	1 Thessalonians
2Jn	2 John	2Th	2 Thessalonians
3Jn	3 John	1Tm	1 Timothy
Jon	Jonah	2Tm	2 Timothy
Jos	Joshua	Tt	Titus
Jude	Jude	Tb	Tobit
Jg	Judges	Ws	Wisdom
Jdt	Judith	Ze	Zechariah
		Zp	Zephaniah

APPENDIX 1

THE VERSES OF SCRIPTURE IN THE ROSARY

THE SIGN OF THE CROSS: In the name of the Father, and
of the Son, and of the Holy Spirit. Amen. Matthew 28:19   1

TOTAL VERSES OF SCRIPTURE IN "SIGN OF THE CROSS" 1

THE ANNOUNCEMENT OF THE HOLY ROSARY:
He came unto His own,
His own received Him not. But to as many as received Him
He gave the power of becoming sons of God. Jn 1:11,12   2

TOTAL VERSES OF SCRIPTURE ANNOUNCING ROSARY 2

THE CREED: I believe in God, the Father Almighty, Jn 14:1   1
the Creator of heaven and earth; Gn 1:1   1
and in Jesus Christ His only Son, Our Lord; Ac 8:37   1
Who was conceived by the Holy Spirit,
born of the Virgin Mary, Lk 1:35   1
suffered under Pontius Pilate, Mk 15:15   1
was crucified, Mk 15:24   1
died, Mk 15:37   1
and was buried. Mk 15:46   1
He descended into hell; 1P 3:19   1
the third day He arose again from the dead; Mk 16:6   1
He ascended into heaven, sitteth at the right hand of God,
the Father Almighty; Mk 16:19   1
from thence He shall come to judge the living
and the dead. Ac 10:42   1
I believe in the Holy Spirit, Jn 14:26   1
the Holy Catholic Church, Mt 16:18   1
the communion of saints, Mk 9:3   1
the forgiveness of sins, Jn 20:23   1
the resurrection of the body, Lk 14:14   1
and life everlasting. Amen. Jn 3:16   1

TOTAL VERSES OF SCRIPTURE IN THE "CREED"   18

THE LORD'S PRAYER: Our Father Who art in heaven,
hallowed be Thy name. Mt 6:9   1
Thy kingdom come, Thy will be done on earth,
as it is in heaven. Mt 6:10   1
Give us this day our daily bread. Mt 6:11   1
And forgive us our trespasses,
as we forgive those who trespass against us. Mt 6:12   1
And lead us not into temptation,
but deliver us from evil. Amen. Mt 6:13   1

TOTAL VERSES OF SCRIPTURE IN THE "LORD'S PRAYER" 5

THE HAIL MARY: Hail Mary, full of grace! The Lord is
with thee; blessed art thou amongst women, Lk 1:28   1
and blessed is the fruit of thy womb, Jesus. Lk 1:42   1
Holy Mary, Mother of God, Lk 1:43   1
pray for us sinners, Jm 5:16   1
now and at the hour of our death. Amen.

TOTAL VERSES OF SCRIPTURE IN THE "HAIL MARY"   4

GLORY be to the Father, and to the Son, Jn 17:5   1
and to the Holy Spirit, Jn 4:23   1
as it was in the beginning, is now, and ever shall be,
world without end. Amen. Hb 13:8   1

TOTAL VERSES OF SCRIPTURE IN THE "GLORY BE"   3

THE JOYFUL MYSTERIES.
The Annunciation. Lk 1:28   1
The Visitation. Lk 1:39   1
The Birth of Jesus. Lk 2:7   1
The Presentation. Lk 2:22   1
The Finding of the Child Jesus in the Temple. Lk 2:46   1

THE SORROWFUL MYSTERIES.
The Agony in the garden. Mt 26:38   1
The Scourging at the pillar. Jn 19:1   1
The Crowning with thorns. Mt 27:29   1
The Carrying of the Cross. Jn 19:17   1
The Death on the Cross. Jn 19:30   1

THE GLORIOUS MYSTERIES.

The Resurrection. Mk 16:6	1
The Ascension. Lk 24:51	1
The Descent of the Holy Spirit. Ac 2:3	1
The Assumption. Sg 6:10	1
The Coronation. 1P 5:4	1

TOTAL VERSES OF SCRIPTURE IN THE "MYSTERIES"   15

THE ORDER OF THE ROSARY IS:

1	Sign of the Cross	1
1	Creed	18
1	Our Father	5
3	"Hail Marys"	12
1	Glory be to the Father	3
1	Announcement of the Rosary	2
3	Titles of the Mysteries	15
15	"Our Fathers"	75
150	"Hail Marys"	600
15	"Glorys"	45
1	Sign of the Cross	1

TOTAL VERSES OF SCRIPTURE IN THE ROSARY   777

APPENDIX 2

THE MESSAGES OF FATIMA

Relayed trough the three children visionaries, Lucia, Francisco and Jacinta.

13 May 1917. "I come from Heaven. I want you to come here at this same hour on the 13th day of each month until October. Then I will tell you who I am and what I want."

13 June 1917. "God wishes you to remain in the world for some time because He wants to use you to establish in the world the devotion to my Immaculate Heart. I promise salvation to those who embrace it, and their souls will be loved by God as flowers placed by myself to adorn His throne."

13 July 1917. During her appearance Our Lady promised that she would work a great public miracle in October so that all people might believe and know who she was. She also told the children to offer sacrifices for sinners, and to say many times, "O my Jesus, I offer this for love of Thee, for the conversion of sinners, and in reparation for all the sins committed against the Immaculate Heart of Mary."

She showed the children Hell and all the devils and sinners tumbling and tossing without rest in the fire. Their bodies were on fire within and without and never an instant of peace. Our Lady said to the children, "You have seen Hell, where the souls of poor sinners go. To save them, God wishes to establish in the world the devotion to my Immaculate Heart. If people do what tell you, many souls will be saved and there will be peace."

"The war (WW I was then being fought) is going to end. But if people do not stop offending God, another and worse one will begin in the reign of Pius XI (1922-1939). When you shall see a night illuminated by an unknown light (this was seen on 25 January 1938) know that this is the great sign that God gives you that He is going to punish the world for its many crimes by means of war, hunger and persecution of the Church and the Holy Father. To prevent this, I shall come to ask for the consecration of Russia to my Immaculate Heart and the Communion of Reparation on the five first Saturdays. If my requests are granted, Russia will be converted and there will be peace. If not, she will scatter her errors throughout the world, provoking wars and persecution of the Church. The good will be martyred, the Holy Father will have much to suffer, and various nations will be destroyed."

The next part of the message was to be kept secret until our Blessed Mother gave permission for it to be revealed.

"But in the end, my Immaculate Heart will triumph, the Holy Father will consecrate Russia to me, Russia will be converted, and a certain period of peace will be granted to the world."

13 August 1917. The children were kidnapped and jailed by the mayor of fatima. Our lady appeared to he children on 19 August 1917 near the village of Valinhos. She told them she was greatly displeased by the action of the mayor.

13 September 1917. Over 30,000 were present and saw a shower of mysterious white petals fall and dissolve into thin air when they were about 10 feet from the ground

13 October 1917. "I am the Lady of the Rosary. I have come to warn the faithful to amend their lives and to ask pardon for their sins. They must not offend Our Lord any more, for He is already too grievously offended by the sins of men. people must say the Rosary. Let them continue saying it every day. Add after each decade the following prayer: 'O my Jesus, forgive us our sins, save us from the fires of Hell, lead all souls to Heaven, especially those who have most need of Thy mercy."

On that day about 60,000 people witnessed the sun spin and dance and seemed to come down to earth. The rain drenched people and ground were instantly dried.

SUBSEQUENT EVENTS

Before she died in February 1920, Jacinta revealed some remarkable statements made by our Blessed Mother.

"More souls go to Hell because of sins of the flesh than for any other reason."

"Certain fashions will be introduced that will offend Our Lord very much."

"Many marriages are not good; the do not please Our Lord and are not of God."

132

"Priests must be pure, very pure. They should not busy themselves with anything except what concerns the Church and souls. The disobedience of priests to their superiors and to the Holy Father is very displeasing to Our Lord."

"The Blessed Mother can no longer restrain the hand of her Divine Son from striking the world with just punishment for its many crimes."

"If the government of a country leaves the Church in peace and gives liberty to our Holy Religion, it will be blessed by God."

"Tell everybody that God gives graces through the Immaculate Heart of Mary. Tell them to ask graces from her, and that the Heart of Jesus wishes to be venerated together with the Immaculate Heart of Mary. Ask them to plead for peace from the Immaculate Heart of Mary, for the Lord has confided the peace of the world to her."

10 December 1925. To Lucia, now Sister Lucia, the Blessed Mother and the Child Jesus appeared to her. Jesus said,

"Have pity on the heart of your Most Holy Mother. It is covered with thorns with which ungrateful men pierce it at every moment, and there is no one to remove them with a act of reparation."
Holding in her hand, a heart surrounded with sharp thorns, Our Lady said, "My child, behold my heart surrounded with thorns which ungrateful men place therein at every moment by their blasphemies and ingratitude. You at least try to console me. Announce in my name that I promise to assist at the hour of death with all graces necessary for salvation, all those who, on the first Saturday of five consecutive months, go to Confession and receive Holy Communion, recite the Rosary, and keep me company for fifteen minutes while meditating on the mysteries of the Rosary, with the intention of making reparation to me."

In 1929 Our Lady appeared to Sister Lucia and gave her permission to reveal the secrets outlined above which were:
The vision of Hell.
The prediction of another war.
Martyrdom for Christians.
The destruction of nations.
The persecution of the Church and the Holy Father.
The spread of Communism.
The devotion to the Immaculate Heart of Mary.

133

In 1929 Our Lady appeared again to Sister Lucia and completed the promise to ask for the consecration of Russia to the Immaculate Heart of Mary and the Communion of Reparation on the First Saturdays.

"The moment has come in which God asks the Holy Father, in union with all the bishops of the world, to make the consecration of Russia to my Immaculate Heart, promising to save it by this means. There are so many souls whom the justice of God condemns for sins committed against me, that I have come to ask reparation; sacrifice yourself for this intention and pray."

APPENDIX 3

RESOLUTION 666 (SEPTEMBER 13, 1990)

The Security Council,
Recalling its resolution 661 (1990), paragraphs 3 (c) and 4 of which apply, except in humanitarian circumstances, to foodstuffs,
Recognizing that circumstances may arise in which it will be necessary for foodstuffs to be supplied to civilian population in Iraq or Kuwait in order to relieve human suffering,
Noting that in this respect the Committee established under paragraph 6 of that resolution has received communications from several Member States,
Emphasizing that it is for the Security Council, alone or acting through the Committee, to determine whether humanitarian circumstances have arisen,
Deeply concerned that Iraq has failed to comply with its obligations under Security Council resolution 664 (1990) in respect of the safety and well-being of third State nationals, and reaffirming that Iraq retains full responsibility in this regard under international humanitarian law including, where applicable, the Fourth Geneva Convention,
Acting under Chapter VII of the Charter of the United Nations,

1. **Decides** that in order to make the necessary determination whether or not for the purposes of paragraph 3 (c) and paragraph 4 of resolution 661 (1990) humanitarian circumstances have arisen, the Committee shall keep the situation regarding foodstuffs in Iraq and Kuwait under constant review;
2. **Expects** Iraq to comply with its obligations under Security Council resolution 664 (1990) in respect of third State nationals and reaffirms that Iraq remains fully responsible for their safety and well-being in accordance with international humanitarian law including, where applicable, the Fourth Geneva Convention;
3. **Requests**, for the purposes of paragraphs 1 and 2 of this resolution, that the Secretary-General seek urgently, and on a continuing basis, information from relevant United Nations and other appropriate humanitarian agencies and all other sources on the availability of food in Iraq and Kuwait, such information to be communicated by the Secretary-General to the Committee regularly;
4. **Requests** further that in seeking and supplying such information particular attention will be paid to such categories of persons who might suffer specially, such as children under 15 years of age, expectant mothers, maternity cases, the sick and the elderly;
5. **Decides** that if the Committee, after receiving reports from the Secretary-General, determines that circumstances have arisen in which there

is an urgent humanitarian need to supply foodstuffs to Iraq or Kuwait in order to relieve human suffering, it will report promptly to the Council its decision as to how such need should be met;

6. Directs the Committee that in formulating its decisions it should bear in mind that foodstuffs should be provided through the United Nations in co-operation with the International Committee of the Red Cross or other appropriate humanitarian agencies and distributed by them or under their supervision in order to ensure that they reach the intended beneficiaries;

7. Requests the Secretary-General to use his good offices to facilitate the delivery and distribution of foodstuffs to Kuwait and Iraq in accordance with the provisions of this and other relevant resolutions;

8. Recalls that resolution 661 (1990) does not apply to supplies intended strictly for medical purposes, but in this connection recommends that medical supplies should be exported under strict supervision of the Government of the exporting State or by appropriate humanitarian agencies.

VOTE: 13 for, 0 against, 2 abstentions (Cuba and Yemen).

Source: US Department of State Dispatch. September 24, 1990. p 112.

APPENDIX 4

Declaration on the Elimination of All Forms of Intolerance and of Discrimination Based on Religion or Belief

The General Assembly,

Considering that one of the basic principles of the Charter of the United Nations is that of the dignity and equality inherent in all human beings, and that all Member States have pledged themselves to take joint and separate action in cooperation with the United Nations to promote and encourage universal respect for and observance of human rights and fundamental freedoms for all, without distinction as to race, sex, language or religion,

Considering that the Universal declaration of Human Rights and the International Covenants on Human Rights proclaim the principles of non-discrimination and equality before the law and the right to freedom of thought, conscience, religion or belief,

Considering that the disregard and infringement of human rights and fundamental freedoms, in particular of the right to freedom of thought, conscience, religion or whatever belief, have brought, directly or indirectly, wars and great suffering to mankind, especially where they serve as a means of foreign interference in the internal affairs of other States and amount to kindling hatred between peoples and nations,

Considering that religion and belief, for anyone who professes either, is one of the fundamental elements in his conception of life and that freedom of religion should be fully respected and guaranteed,

Considering that it is essential to promote understanding, tolerance and respect in matters relating to freedom of religion or belief and to ensure that the use of religion or belief for ends inconsistent with the Charter, other relevant instruments of the United Nations and the purposed and principles of the present Declaration is inadmissible,

Convinced that freedom of religion or belief should also contribute to the attainment of the goals of world peace, social justice and friendship among peoples and to the elimination of ideologies or practices of colonialism and racial discrimination,

Noting with satisfaction the adoption of several, and the coming into force of some, conventions, under the aegis of the United Nations and of the specialized agencies, for the elimination of various forms of discrimination,

Concerned by manifestations of intolerance and by the existence of discrimination in matters of religion or belief still in evidence in some areas of the world,

Resolved to adopt all necessary measures for a speedy elimination of such intolerance in all its forms and manifestations and to prevent and combat discrimination on the grounds of religion or belief,

Proclaims this Declaration on the Elimination of All Forms of Intolerance and of Discrimination Based on Religion or Belief:

Article 1

1.   Everyone shall have the right to freedom of thought, conscience and religion. This right shall include freedom to have religion or whatever belief of his choice, and freedom, either individually or in community with others and in public or private, to manifest his religion or belief in worship, observance, practice and teaching.

2.   No one shall be subject to coercion which would impair his freedom to have a religion or belief of hid choice.

3.   Freedom to manifest one's religion or belief may be subject only to such limitations as are prescribed by law and are necessary to protect public safety, order, health or morals or the fundamental rights and freedoms of others.

Article 2

1.   No one shall be subject to discrimination by any State, Institution, group of persons or person on the grounds of religious belief.

2.   For the purposes of the present Declaration, the expression "intolerance and discrimination based on religion or belief" means by distinction, exclusion, restriction or preference based on religion or belief and having as its purpose or as its effect nullification or impairment of the recognition, enjoyment or exercise of human rights and fundamental freedoms on an equal basis.

Article 3

Discrimination between human beings on the grounds of religion or belief constitutes an affront to human dignity and a disavowal of the principles of the Charter of the United Nations, and shall be condemned as a violation of the human rights and fundamental freedoms proclaimed in the Universal Declaration of Human Rights and enunciated in detail in the International Covenants on Human Rights, and as an obstacle to friendly and peaceful relations between nations.

Article 4

1.   All States shall take effective measures to prevent and eliminate discrimination on the grounds of religion or belief in the recognition, exercise and enjoyment of human rights and fundamental freedoms in all fields of civil, economic, political, social and cultural life.

2. All States shall make all efforts to enact or rescind legislation where necessary to prohibit any such discrimination, and to take all appropriate measures to combat intolerance on the grounds of religion or belief in this matter.

Article 5

1. The parents or, as the case may be, the legal guardians of the child have the right to organize the life within the family in accordance with their religion or belief and bearing in mind the moral education in which they believe the child should be brought up.
2. Every child shall enjoy the right to have access to education in the matter of religion or belief in accordance with the wishes of his parents or, as the case may be, legal guardians, and shall not be compelled to receive teaching on religion or belief against the wishes of his parents or legal guardians, the best interests of the child being the guiding principle.
3. The child shall be protected from any form of discrimination on the grounds of religion or belief. He shall be brought up in a spirit of understanding, tolerance, friendship among peoples, peace, and universal brotherhood, respect for freedom of religion or belief of others, and in full consciousness that his energy and talents should be devoted to the service of his fellow man.
4. In the case of a child who is under the care either of his parents or of legal guardians, due account shall be taken of their expressed wishes or of any other proof of their wishes in the matter of religion or belief, the best interests of the child being the guiding principle.
5. Practices of a religion or belief in which a child is brought up must not be injurious to his physical or mental health or to his full development, taking into account article 1, paragraph 3, of the present Declaration.

Article 6

In accordance with article 1, paragraph 3, the right to freedom of thought, conscience, religion or belief shall include inter alia, the following freedoms:

(a) To worship or assemble in connection with a religion or belief, and to establish and maintain places for these purposes;

(b) To establish and maintain appropriate charitable humanitarian institutions;

(c) To make, acquire and use to an adequate extent the necessary articles and materials related to the rites or customs of a religion or belief;

(d) To write, issue and disseminate relevant publications in these areas;

(e) To teach a religion or belief in places suitable for these purposes;

(f) To solicit and receive voluntary financial and other contributions from individuals and institutions;

(g) To train, appoint, elect or designate by succession appropriate leaders called for by the requirements and standards of any religion or belief;

(h) To observe days of rest and to celebrate holidays and ceremonies in accordance with the precepts of one's religion or belief;

(i) To establish and maintain communications with individuals and communities in matters of religion or belief at the national and international levels.

Article 7

The rights and freedoms set forth in the present Declaration shall be accorded in national legislations in such a manner that everyone shall be able to avail himself of such rights and freedoms in practice.

Article 8

Nothing in the present Declaration shall be construed as restricting or derogating from any right defined in the Universal Declaration of Human Rights and the   International Covenants on Human Rights.

General Assembly decision 36/412
Adopted without vote.

ENDNOTES

All quotations are from the Douay Rheims Bible except where noted (NJB), these being from the New Jerusalem Bible. Where differences in verse numbering occurs between the Vulgate and Hebrew editions I have included by bracketing the alternative numbering.

1. Phm 4,5
2. Jm 5:16
3. Gobbi, p 691a
4. Lv 25:10
5. Gobbi, p 615b, 616d
6. Is 58:12(NJB)
7. 1Ch 28:20
8. Ps 125:2(126:2)
9. Ps 149: 5-9
10. Ep 1:9
11. Gn 1:1
12. Re 12:7,8
13. Jb 1:6
14. Jb 1:7
15. Gn 3:15
16. Lk 2:35
17. Gn 6:9
18. Lk 3:23-38
19. Gn 28:12-14
20. Gn 27:29
21. Nu 24:17
22. Is 7:14
23. Is 9:6
24. Is 9:8
25. Farrell and Kosiki, p. 49
26. Lk 1:28,35
27. Re 8:1
28. Lk 1:38
29. Lk 4:3
30. 1Co 2:7,8
31. Jn 19:26,27
32. Jos 3:16 and 1P 3:19
33. Heb 9:4
34. Ezk 43:2-7; 44:2

35. Re 2:28; 22:16
36. 1Co 15:41
37. Mt 2:10
38. 1Co 3:16
39. Rm 12:5
40. 1Co 11:3
41. Sg 6:9
42. Jdt 13:22-24, 31
43. Lk 1:46-48
44. 2Th 2:15
45. Is 26:19
46. Dn 12:2-3
47. Mt 27:52
48. Jn 2:5
49. Ex 24:8
50. Mt 26:26-28
51. Ps 2:6
52. 1K 8:1
53. Si 36:15 (12 in NJB)
54. Is 60:14
55. Mt 16:19
56. Rm 1:8-17
57. Gn 18:2,3
58. Mt 28:19
59. 1P 1:2
60. Is 11:1
61. Mt 1:1-16
62. Zc 6:12
63. Col 1:18
64. Mt 9:37
65. Jn 2:19,21
66. 2Co 3:14 (NJB)
67. Mt 5:17
68. Lv 4:6,16,17

69. Ps 22:16-31(NJB), (21:17-32)
70. Is 31:5
71. 2Th 2:3-6
72. Lv 27:25
73. Ezk 38:12
74. 2Th 2:4
75. Dn 12:10
76. Re 17:5
77. 1Tm 6:10
78. Fisher, p D-7
79. Epperson, p. 145
80. Ws 11:21
81. Hardon, p. 381, 382
82. Ps 58:4 and 59:8
83. Lk 16:9
84. Mt 11:12
85. Nu 21:5-9
86. 2Co 12:10
87. Ps 32:8, 33:18, 94:9
88. Is 40:31
89. Pr 23:5
90. Ps 103:5
91. Nu 22:28
92. 1M 1:18
93. Gn 41:32
94. 1Co 12:4-11
95. Ga 5:22
96. Sg 4:11-14
97. Ex 4:6
98. Ps 147:8, 108:4, 104:3
99. Lk 21:27
100. Ac 1:11
101. Heb 2:11
102. Phil 1:6
103. Re 14:7
104. Re 14:8
105. Re 14:9-11
106. Re 21:1,2
107. Gn 10:10
108. Gn 11:3-9
109. Dn 4:27
110. Is 13:11-20
111. Is 47:5-9

112. Jr 51:6-13
113. Jr 51:27
114. Gn 2:11
115. Gn 13:2
116. Gn 23:16
117. Ex 30:13
118. Ezk 45:12
119. Lv 19:35, 36
120. Am 8:4-7
121. 1Co 5:6
122. La 3:34-36 (NJB)
123. Is 1: 21-26
124. Mt 15:13
125. Mk 8:15
126. Lv 26:11, 12
127. Dt 17:14-20 (NJB)
128. 1S 8:11-18 (NJB)
129. Ne 5:4,5 (NJB)
130. Ne 5:15 (NJB)
131. Ezk 45:9 (NJB)
132. Hg 1:6 (NJB)
133. Lv 17:35 (NJB)
134. Pr 11:1 (NJB)
135. Re 18:3,6 (NJB)
136. Ps 9:15 (NJB), 9:16
137. Allen, p. 50
138. Ho 4:6 (NJB)
139. Is 30:6 (NJB)
140. Is 10:1-4 (NJB)
141. 1Co 2:6 (NJB)
142. Dn 11:43
143. Ex 22:25-27 (NJB)
144. Lv 25:35-37 (NJB)
145. Dt 23:19 (NJB)
146. Ne 5:1-7, 13 (NJB)
147. Pr 28:8 (NJB)
148. 2Co 8:12 (NJB)
149. Jr 15:10 (NJB)
150. Pr 22:7
151. Re 6:6 (NJB)
152. Hab 3:16 (NJB)
153. Re 13:2 (NJB)
154. 1Jn 2: 18 (NJB)

155. Lk 21:34 (NJB)
156. Is 4:6 (NJB)
157. Is 43:19
158. Jl 2:28 (3:1 NJB)
159. Ho 12:10
160. Re 12:1
161. Mt 21:16
162. Gobbi, 14 May 89 e
163. Gobbi, 3 Jun 89 d
164. Gobbi, 13 Jun 89 f,g
165. Jr 6:14
166. Re 12:3
167. Re 13:1-4
168. Gn 1:26
169. 1Co 6:3
170. Jr 17:18
171. Jr 6:19
172. Ac 2:41
173 Ac 6:7
174. Jn 21:25
175. Graham, p. 106
176. 1Co 1:23
177. New Catholic Ency. p. 395
178. Re: 10:4
179. Re 17:9
180. Re 13:4
181. Re 16:12-14, 16
182. Ezk 38:4-6
183. Ezk 38:18-22
184. Zp 1:10,11(NJB)
185. Ep 6:12
186. 1Jn 5:5
187. Pr 9:1
188. Dn 11:36
189. Re 13:13
190. Gn 3:1-5
191. Jr 51:30
192. Re 13:3
193. 1M 2:49 (NJB)
194. Mt 16:18
195. Re 11:15
196. Re 2:26
197. Mk 5:21-43

198. 2Ch 7:14
199. Pr 21:12
200. Ws 6:1-7
201. 1Tm 2:1-4(NJB)
202. Rm 13:1(NJB)
203. Tt 3:1-3(NJB)
204. 1P 2:13-15,17
205. Is 25:4
206. 2S 22:26-28 (NJB)
207. Re 17:16-18
208. Re 13:18
209. 2Th 2:8
210. Re 13:11,12
211. Ex 28:4
212. Jg 21:24
213. Re 3:9
214. Ezk 22:24,25
215. Jg 17:6
216. Re 2:8,9
217. UN Yearbook 1981. p.881
218. Dn 12:11
219. 1Co 11:25
220. Mt 24:15-22
221. Gn 7:6,11,13 (NJB)
222. Gn 6:5-10 (NJB)
223. Gn 8:13 (NJB)
224. Gn 49:1,17 (NJB)
225. Epperson, p. 40-41
226. Dt 33:22 (NJB)
227. Jg 1:34 (NJB)
228. Jg 16-17
229. Jg 18:18,30 (NJB)
230. Jg 18:27,28 (NJB)
231. Jg 17:7,8 (NJB)
232. Jr 8:16,17 (NJB)
233. Dn 3:1-6 (NJB)
234. Gn 1:26-31
235. Lk 10:13-15
236. Re 13 (NJB)
237. Re 7:2-8 (NJB)
238. Gobbi, p. 655, 656
239. Gobbi, 13 Mar 90 b,d
240. Gobbi, 31 Dec 84 l

241. Gobbi, 26 Jun 91 f	284. Lk 16:19-31
242. Jl 2:1	285. Jn 19:27
243. Am 5:18-20	286. Jb 1:21
244. Ml 4:1	287. Rm 11:25
245. 1M 9:25 (NJB)	288. Jn 10:1
246. 2Jn 8	289. Mt 24:10 (NJB)
247. Dn 9:27 (NJB)	290. Re 2:4,14,20-22 (NJB)
248. Re 21:2	291. Gn 38:9,10
249. Obd 4 (NJB)	292. Tb 4:13
250. 2M 6:12 (NJB)	293. Mt 14:15-17
251. Es 11:5-8	294. 1Th 4:15-17
252. Is 26:20	295. Pr 10:30
253. Is 26:21	296. 1Co 15:51,52
254. Gn 25:33	297. Re 6:12-13
255. Jr 14:3	298. Gn 41:28-32
256. Ba 4:21 (NJB)	299. Ezr 8:22
257. Gobbi, 29 sep 90 h	300. Is 11:11,& 49:22 (NJB)
258. 2Th 1:6-10	301. Is 40:10 (NJB)
259. 2M 5:2-4 (NJB)	302. Is 49:19
260. Gobbi, 1 Nov 90 e	303. Is 49:10-13
261. Es 5:11;6:12,13	304. Zc 6:13
262. Ml 4:2,3	305. Is 8:14 (NJB)
263. Gobbi, 15 Sep 90 f	306. Dt 32:21
264. Jon 4:2 (NJB)	307. Is 65:1,2
265. Re 18:4	308. Lk 9:28-33
266. Re 7:3	309. Ps 74:10 (NJB)
267. Is 11:11,12	310. Es 7:1-7
268. Dn 3:24	311. Is 53:2-5
269. Jn 10:16	312. Jn 17:3,10,21,22
270. Ep 1:3,8,9	313. Re 22:12-15
271. Mk 9:39	314. Eccl 7:9
272. Tt 3:15	315. Gobbi, 3 Jun 90 e
273. Jn 6:67	316. Mt 28:18
274. Lk 8:25	317. Phil 2:15,16(NJB)
275. Lk 18:8	318. Ps 15 & Is 57:13
276. Lk 10:16	319. Gobbi, 16 Oct 91 p,q
277. Lk 11:28	320. Mt 5:4
278. Mt 12:47	321. Re 17:14
279. Ps 50:20 (NJB)	322. Is 55:11
280. Lk 9:29	323. Is 10:20-23
281. Dt 34:5	324. Is 43:2
282. 2K 2:11	325. Mi 5:7 (NJB)
283. Mal 3:23 (NJB), (4:5)	326. Jn 5:28,29

327. Rt 2:20
328. 2M 12:40-45 (NJB)
329. Re 12:6
330. Lk 14:14
331. Gobbi, 1 Jan 90 f-h
332. Mt 24:36
333. Re 20:1-10
334. Mt. 10:7
335. Lk 17:20,21
336. Lk 9:27
337. Gobbi, 5 Mar 82 d
338. Gobbi, 31 Aug 88 p
339. Gobbi, 30 Mar 86 g
340. Gobbi, 1 Jan 90 b,h,i
341. Ps 110:1
342. 1Co 15:24,25
343. Gobbi, 1 Jan 79 h,i
344. Gobbi, 6 Sep 86 h
345. Gobbi, 15 Aug 88 e
346. 2Jn 7,9-11 (NJB)
347. Pr 3:5
348. 3Jn 11
349. Gobbi, 8 Jun 91 d
350. Gobbi, 15 Nov 90 d
351. Gobbi, 12 Sep 91 f
352. Gobbi, 8 Sep 78 h
353. Re 12:5
354. Mk 10:45
355. Re 1:10,19
356. Re 12:4
357. Gobbi, 8 Dec 79 l
358. 2Th 2:3-8(NJB)
359. Gobbi, 13 May 90 f-i
360. Gobbi, 13 Oct 90 f
361. Gobbi, 1 Nov 89 h
362. Gobbi, 13 May 91 f
363. Ep 2:4-9
364. Rm 4:13
365. Ho 2:5
366. Gobbi, 13 Oct 91 e,h
367. Gobbi, 7 Oct 83 h
368. Ps 26:14 (27:14)
369. 1Th 5:17-22

370. Gobbi, 1 May 88 e
371. Gobbi, 22 May 88 a-d
372. Gobbi, 7 Oct 90 h
373. Mt 5:18
374. Gobbi, 19 May 91 f,g
375. Gobbi, 13 Oct 90 b-d
376. Re 21:3
377. Gobbi, 26 Feb 91 u,x
378. Gobbi, 12 Apr 90 m.n
379. Gobbi, 8 Dec 90 e
380. Lk 1:38
381. Gobbi, 24 Dec 78 e-j
382. Gobbi, 25 Mar 89 k
383. Mt 18:14
384. Gobbi, 3 Jul 87 s,t
385. Gobbi, 24 Dec 89 o
386. Ps 103:30(102:30)
387. Gobbi, 23 Jun 90 l
388. Gobbi, 3 Jun 90 a-l
389. Lv 25:10,11
390. Gobbi, 24 Dec 91 g,j
391. Gobbi, 15 Aug 91 a
392. Gobbi, 26 Jun 91 i
393. Jn 5:3
394. Gobbi, 26 Mar 89 b-g
395. Gobbi, 8 Sep 90 a-l
396. Gobbi, 8 Dec 90 e-l
397. Gobbi, 24 Dec 90 f,g
398. Gobbi, 15 Apr 90 f,g
399. Gobbi, 13 May 91 g
400. Gobbi, 30 Mar 91 e
401. Ps 103:1,2 (104:1,2)
402. Jb 38:7
403. 2Co 12:2
404. 2P 3:5-13
405. 1Co 7:31
406. Jb 34:20
407. Na 1:12(NJB)
408. Ep 4:14
409. Lk 21:32,33
410. Re 21:1
411. 2P 3:14
412. Gn 2:25

413. Gn 3:7	438. 1Co 15:21-24
414. Gn 3:23,24	439. 1Co 15:42-57
415. Gn 5:1-3	440. Mt 9:16
416. Mk 2:18-21	441. Ga 1:11,12
417. Lk 5:37-39	442. Col 1:15-19
418. 1Jn 2:16-19	443. Col 2:9
419. Re 19:1-8	444. Col 2:10-12
420. Ep 5:27	445. Ep 3:16-19
421. 1P 3:3,4	446. Ep 4:12-14
422. 1P 1:4,5	447. 2P 1:3-4
423. Rm 5:12,20,21	448. 2Co 4:7
424. Rm 4:17	449. 1P 5:10,11
425. Rm 6:6,7,12	450. 2Co 4:4
426. Rm 6:14,22	451. 2P 2:20-22
427. Rm 7:14-25	452. Re 3:2-6
428. Phil 3:12	453. Re 3:18
429. Ep 4:20-24	454. Heb 12:5,6
430. Col 3:4-6,9,12-14	455. Re 16:13-16
431. 2Co 5:1-4	456. Jn 14:12
432. Lk 21:27,28	457. Phil 4:12,13
433. 2Co 3:18	458. 2P 2:1-3
434. 1Co 15:45	459. Tt 1:10,15,16
435. 2Co 4:3-4	460. 2Tm 2:23
436. 2Co 5:5,8-10	461. Zc 9:12
437. 2Co 5:17	462. Jude 25(NJB)

PRAYER TO JESUS

Behold O kind and Most Sweet Jesus,
I cast myself upon my knees in Thy sight,
And with the most fervent desire of my soul,
I pray and beseech Thee,
That Thou wouldst impress upon my heart,
Lively sentiments of faith, hope and charity,
A true contrition for my sins
And a firm purpose of amendment.
Whilst with deep affection and grief of soul,
I ponder within myself
And mentally contemplate Thy five most precious wounds,
Having before my eyes
The words which David Thy prophet said concerning Thee,
They have pierced My hands and My feet,
They have numbered all My bones.

PRAYER TO SAINT JOSEPH

O, Saint Joseph, whose protection is so great, so strong,
so prompt before the throne of God,
I place in you all my interest and desires.
O, Saint Joseph, do assist me by your powerful intercession,
and obtain for me from your divine Son all spiritual blessings,
through Jesus Christ our Lord.
So that, having engaged here below your heavenly power,
I may offer my thanksgiving and homage to the most loving of Fathers.
O, Saint Joseph, I never weary contemplating you,
and Jesus asleep in your arms;
I dare not approach while He reposes near your heart.
Press Him in my name and kiss His fine head for me
and ask Him to return the kiss when I draw my dying breath.
Saint Joseph, Patron of departing souls, pray for me.

PRAYER TO SAINT MICHAEL THE ARCHANGEL

SEE Page 99

LITANY OF THE BLESSED VIRGIN MARY

Lord, have mercy on us.
Christ have mercy on us.
Lord, have mercy on us.
Christ hear us.
Christ graciously hear us.
God the Father of Heaven,
Have mercy on us.
God the Son, Redeemer of the world,
Have mercy on us.
God the Holy Ghost, *Have mercy on us.*
Holy Trinity, one God,*Have mercy on us.*
Holy Mary, *pray for us.*
Holy Mother of God, *pray for us*
Holy Virgin of virgins, *etc.*
Mother of Christ,
Mother of divine grace,
Mother most pure,
Mother most chaste,
Mother inviolate,
Mother undefiled.,
Mother most amiable,
Mother most admirable,
Mother of good counsel,
Mother of our Creator,
Mother of our Savior,
Virgin most prudent,
Virgin most venerable,
Virgin most renowned,
Virgin most powerful,
Virgin most merciful,
Virgin most faithful,
Mirror of justice,
Seat of wisdom,
Cause of our joy,
Spiritual vessel,
Vessel of honor,
Singular vessel of devotion,
Mystical rose,
Tower of David,
Tower of ivory, *etc.*

House of gold, *pray etc.*
Ark of the Covenant,
Gate of Heaven,
Morning Star,
Health of the sick,
Refuge of sinners,
Comforter of the afflicted,
Help of Christians,
Queen of angels,
Queen of patriarchs,
Queen of prophets,
Queen of apostles,
Queen of martyrs,
Queen of confessors,
Queen of virgins,
Queen of saints,
Queen conceived without original sin,
Queen assumed into Heaven,
Queen of the most holy Rosary,
Queen of peace,

Lamb of God, Who takest away the sins
the world, Spare us, O Lord.
Lamb of God, who takest away the sins
the world, Graciously hear us, O Lord.
Lamb of God, Who takest away the sins
the world, Have mercy on us.

Pray for us, O Holy Mother of God, Th
we may be made worthy the promises
Christ.

Let us pray.
Pour forth, we beseech Thee, O Lord, Th
grace into our hearts, that we through whor
the incarnation of Christ, Thy Son, w
made known by the message of an angel. B
His Passion and Cross, may we be broug
to the glory of His Resurrection, through th
same Christ our Lord. Amen.

ACT OF CONSECRATION
TO THE
IMMACULATE HEART OF MARY

Virgin of Fatima, Mother of Mercy, Queen of Heaven and Earth, Refuge of Sinners, we who belong to the Marian Movement consecrate ourselves in a very special way to your Immaculate Heart.

By this act of consecration we intend to live, with you and through you, all the obligations assumed by our baptismal consecration. We further pledge to bring about in ourselves that interior conversion so urgently demanded by the Gospel, a conversion that will free us from every attachment to ourselves and to easy compromises with the world so that, like you, we may be available only to do always the Will of the Father.

And as we resolve to entrust to you, O Mother most sweet and merciful, our life and vocation as Christians, that you may dispose of it according to your designs of salvation in this hour of decision that weighs upon the world, we pledge to live it according to your desires, especially as it pertains to a renewed spirit of prayer and penance, the fervent participation in the celebration of the Eucharist and in the works of the apostolate, the daily recitation of the holy rosary, and an austere manner of life in keeping with the Gospel, that shall be to all a good example of the observance of the law of God and the practice of the Christian virtues, especially that of purity.

We further promise you to be united with the Holy Father, with the hierarchy and with our priests, in order thus to set up a barrier to the growing confrontation directed against the Magisterium, that threatens the very foundation of the Church.

Under your protection, we want moreover to be apostles of this sorely needed unity of prayer and love for the Pope, on whom we invoke your special protection.

And lastly, in so far as is possible, we promise to lead those souls with whom we come in contact to a renewed devotion to you.

Mindful that atheism has caused shipwreck in the faith to a number of the faithful, that desecration has entered into the holy temple of God, and that evil and sin are spreading more and more throughout the world, we make so bold as to lift our eyes trustingly to you, O Mother of Jesus and our merciful and powerful Mother, and we invoke again today and await from you the salvation of all your children, O clement, O loving, O sweet Virgin Mary.

Catholic Evangelism Press, Inc.

P. O. Box 1282
Boca Raton, FL 33429-1282

ORDER FORM

Phone (305) 360-9331

Name _____

Address _____

City _____ ST._____ Zip_____

Phone (____) _____-_____ Purchase Order No._____

Quantity	Item Description	Each	Total
	* How we as Roman Catholics can know, English	.25	
	* How we as Roman Catholics can know, Spanish	.25	
	* Communicating with God, R.D.Foster, English	.07	
	* Communicating with God, R.D.Foster, Spanish	.07	
	* Catholic Businessmans Encounter, Bill Glass	.07	
	* How to have Peace and Fuller Life on Earth	.07	
	* Decide to Forgive, Fr. Robert DeGrandis SSJ	.15	
	* Prayer Card for Christian Commitment	.15	
	In His Image 14'x18' Museum Quality Print	10.00	
	In His Image 14"x18" Canvas textured Print	11.50	
	In His Image 15"x19" Masonite Plaque	16.00	
	In His Image 11.5"x15.5"x1.25" Floating Frame	38.00	
	The Carpenter Cassette, Fr.Jack McGinnis	7.00	
	Evangelism in the World Summary, Pope Paul VI	.50	
	Born Again Catholic Book, Al Boudreau	5.95	
	The Word of God for all Occasions, Paper back	2.45	
	Promesas de Dios, Paper back	2.45	
	Word of God for all Occasions, Leather bound	9.85	
	The Gift of Morning Star By Thomas Aquinas Devlin (Inquire for wholesale prices)	6.95	

Shipping and Handling = $1.00 + 10% of Total
 	
* Discounts on bulk orders of same Item:
    21-50 Copies....10%
    50-500 Copies...20%
    500 up Copies...30%
	Total
	Shipping and Handling
	Discount
	Amount of Invoice
	
	Paid Check No._____

Thank You for Your Order!	Balance Due

Yes, God so loved the world that He gave His only begotten Son. John 3:16